SIGNS OF THE UNIVERSE

A PRACTICAL GUIDE TO SHIFT YOUR STORY

ULLA SUOKKO

WiseWoman

Ulla Suokko / WiseWoman
www.signsoftheuniverse.com

WiseWoman

Copy editing and production by Stephanie Gunning
Cover design by Ulla Suokko
Book Layout © Book Design Templates

Signs of the Universe / Ulla Suokko. —1st ed.

ISBN 978-1-7344739-0-2 (paperback)
ISBN 978-1-7344739-1-9 (kindle ebook)
ISBN 978-1-7344739-2-6 (epub ebook)

To my mom, Eeva, a physics teacher, textbook author, and visual artist: Thank you for your unwavering love and support.
Kiitos, äiti.

CONTENTS

I see you in your highest light.

ONE

AN INVITATION TO PLAY WITH THE UNIVERSE

What if this was the moment your life changed?

How would it feel if, instead of asking for a sign, you said: *"Hello, Universe, how do you wish to flow through me today? Here I am, ready to play."*

This sets you up to be playful, light, and open for anything that might come. Lightness raises your vibration and allows the Universe to flow through with its unlimited supply and support for your dreams.

And by the way, if you are looking for a sign, this is it. In my world, there are no coincidences. You are here for a reason.

Thank you for being here. I am grateful to connect with you.

As you read, please don't take my word for anything. Feel, taste, reflect, play, experiment, discover, and take what resonates with you. Leave the rest.

What if you could be the master of your own story and command the Universe? What follows is a practical guidebook filled with ideas and inspiration on how to focus your energy with crystal clear intention so that you can choose and commit to being the highest version of yourself.

Understanding and reading the signs of the Universe is a way to know yourself more deeply and to trust your inner guidance. In time you will become an expert in the language with which the Universe communicates with you. If you know and trust yourself, you can learn to consciously shift any limiting story standing in the way of your happiness, freedom, and peace.

Why do I talk about the Universe and not God or something else? To me, the word *Universe* represents the Divine, the impossible-to-wrap-your-mind-around, infinite space of potential in a socially neutral, generally agreeable way regardless of any cultural or religious background. You may imagine your insights, guidance, and connection coming from the Universe, God, Goddess, source, the field of possibility, the matrix of potential, your soul, your higher self, your subconscious mind, or anything else that resonates within your heart. In the infinity of all that is, the immensity of creation and oneness, all these names are true, and all are good. There are a hundred thousand names by which we could call it. I fully honor and acknowledge your choice to call it any name that feels perfect and comfortable for you.

It is not my intention to convince you of anything or to convert you to any belief in this book, only to hold a sacred space for your creative imagination, your peace, power, harmony, healing, and joy, so that you can play and communicate with the Universe in your own way. While fascinating scientific data is backing up the information given in this book, it is not my intention to describe a scientific study. My intent is to invite you to an inspirational space wherein you may explore shifting your state of being and reveal the truth of who you are.

Here and now.

When we consider all that is going on in the world, now is a perfect time to embrace consciousness work and personal transformation. We are alive in our specific era in human history for a reason. We are here to answer a call for which we are fully prepared, even if it doesn't always feel like it. I trust you are reading this book because you heard the call and are willing to shift your story, raise the bar, and make a difference.

Transformation work is a privilege for many of us. At times, it can be difficult just to survive. I acknowledge there are life circumstances that may demand your full attention upon occasion. While those are extreme situations, they might touch any of us unannounced. This gives those of us who can commit to raising our vibration more reason to do so. We do it not only for ourselves but also for those who cannot do it themselves at this time.

When you shift, the world shifts.

You have followed your signs here because you are needed in your unique way. Every choice counts. Every action counts. Every small step toward the attainment of your heart's fulfillment and happiness counts. Thank you for being you. Thank you for showing up. Know that you are not alone. You are infinitely supported.

Also, know that we are in this together.

Should you, for any reason, be in a painful situation or feel stuck, my heart goes out to you. Sometimes life is hard and challenging. Playing with the Universe can feel like an impossible or even an irritating suggestion then, I know. Wherever you are, and however you feel, I hold you in your highest light and trust that there is something for you here if you are reading this. Trust the moment. Trust yourself. Trust life. Trust that each situation contains what you need. Move at your own pace. Especially when things are hard, honor yourself. You might need to take small, gentle, forgiving, compassionate, practical, everyday kind of healing steps. Or you might need to make a massive shift in your energy with a powerful act of choice and commitment.

Much more is always possible for you than you can see. There are times when it is best just to be, allowing a nurturing space for the feelings to be felt. Other times, you need to explode the low or limiting energy and take action.

We are innate storytellers. Our minds never cease to plot and tell stories about the world and ourselves, often with great intensity. Our stories carry the vibration of our feelings, beliefs, and points of view. As we repeat the same stories in our heads over and over, we recreate the same reality over and over, though often wondering why nothing ever changes.

Research shows that we think 60,000–70,000 thoughts every day, and about 90 percent of these thoughts are exactly the same as the day before. We think the same thoughts, which trigger the same emotions, which create the same body chemistry. Which again creates more of the same and becomes a story through which we define and easily limit ourselves.

Our brains are wired to find evidence to support our story—our dominant thoughts, beliefs, viewpoints, ideas, values, opinions, and all the feelings behind them. We train our brains and bodies to become vibrational antennae to broadcast our story to the Universe. The energy of the Universe responds to the vibration of the story, creating momentum for its manifestation in physical reality. The story keeps the energy of creation moving.

Sometimes people ask me, "What about wars and climate change and sickness and poverty? Should we be playing with the Universe when there is so much suffering and real problems in the world?"

My answer is a gentle, loving, compassionate, and resounding YES.

Rather than be overwhelmed by the state of the world or continuing to focus on lack in any form, invest your powerful, precious life force energy into creating empowerment, peace, health, wealth, wellness, and intelligent ecological choices and solutions. Anytime you discover something you want to reject, look for its opposite, then focus on bringing that into being.

What if we all gave the world our love and joy and excitement and caring, instead of our judgment, worry, and fear? Wouldn't that be worth choosing?

The Universe always says yes. It says yes to your vibration. No judgment. No conditions. Your personal energy matters, your vibrational contribution matters.

And remember, if you are feeling low, angry, frustrated, overwhelmed, or in need of help, the Universe has no judgment about that either. Feel your feelings. Do something physical to get the steam out and refocus. Life offers plenty of opportunities to push against density. It is part of our human experience. Consider it your workout with a punching bag. Allow space for it, but then be done with it so that it doesn't invade your existence and become a story, with you as its victim.

Being focused on the good is not about being "positive" or denying what's going on in the "real" world. It is about empowerment. About conscious choice. About taking your power back and stepping into your truth and freedom. It is about making a commitment to yourself to be all you can be, use your unique gifts and talents, and reach for your dreams. This is how you can contribute to a better and more beautiful world for yourself and for others.

Change doesn't happen by observing what's wrong. It happens by choosing what's right and truthful. When you are empowered, you are connected. Then you can see with the eyes of clarity, possibility, and love. Any signs of the Universe will then support you on our path.

You can't be sick enough to help the sick or poor enough to help the poor. You help by choosing health, prosperity, love, joy, and flow. You help by being clear, centered, and focused and learning to love, honor, and accept yourself. You make the best choices for yourself and for the world when you embody your highest vibration consciously.

The more fully present you are, the more difference you can make in the world. You can be the instrument of peace, sow love where there is hatred, and bring light to darkness, as the beautiful Prayer of St. Francis proposes.

You don't need to move to India and become Mother Teresa. Or, perhaps you already live in India. You are invited to transform yourself and the world from right where you are. Invest your energy wisely where you have power, where you have a choice. Invest in elevating your vibration beyond any limiting story to the level of the greatest vision of your desired new reality. Commit to what you wish to see expanded in this world. That is how you may join forces with all others who choose to invest in the bank of health, wealth, healing, joy, happiness, good news, good signs, and love. And guess what? This is what miracles are made of. To paraphrase Gregg Braden, one of the leading proponents bridging science and the possibilities of the human spirit, we only call them miracles until we understand that it is a science and technology we all can learn to use.

I invite you to play with the Universe and imagine vividly with feeling, as a child would. Your imagination is a powerful tool for your intuition. It is a bridge to exchange information with the Universe. When you imagine anything with focused energy, you set the wheels of creation in motion.

We often ask for signs when confused and conflicted, but the answers you seek cannot be found in chaos. As you become more adept at pulling yourself out of limiting stories and returning to your center of clarity, your signs will guide you more effectively so that you may choose to focus your energy on your highest vision and commit to creating a new life.

Perhaps it is time to stop seeking and begin finding.

PLAY WITH THE UNIVERSE

I invite you to play with the Universe because playfulness makes you lighter, which means it raises your vibration. An elevated vibrational state means your matrix of possibility expands, and your creative power multiplies. Studies show that you learn and create new neural pathways easier and faster when you play and have fun.

Throughout this book, there are three kinds of activities you can use to play with the Universe and shift your story. These are:

- Intention, meditation, and visualization practices.
- Instant shift tips consisting of practical breath-sound-movement techniques.
- Journaling to shift your story and create your wisdom book.

Sometimes the activities are a combination of all of the above. Play with these techniques and discover new ones.

The idea is to fine-tune yourself as an instrument so that you can command the energies of your Universe and trust your guidance and intuition more fully.

You might want to read through these Play with the Universe sections and come back to them later, or have your journal ready and take a break from reading each time they come along.

The more you engage, the more your life will benefit.

For the journaling activities, choose two notebooks.

A Journal to Shift Your Story

This can be any type of paper or a notebook, where you may journal, answer questions, and jot down quick notes. Here you may clarify ideas, purge your frustrations, complain, ponder possibilities, figure things out, and write drafts of your vision for your life.

Your Wisdom Book

This book will become your treasure trove, an energy tool you can open at any time to receive inspiration and support. Write on the first page: *This book is dedicated to me.* Then, begin collecting inspiring quotes, poems, thoughts, and pictures, if you like. Only uplifting and motivating entries are allowed. This is not so much for journaling as it is for pearls of understanding, inspired ideas, gratitude, and elevated insights.

Energy Follows Intention: Everyday Rituals

As energy follows intention, it is powerful to choose small rituals to clear, cleanse, and invoke with intention.

Another way to say this is: Where attention goes, energy flows.

Rituals done with intention are announcements to the Universe. Use your breath and speak out loud to announce, declare, move, direct, and command the energies.

Clear Your Space

Before you meditate, journal, dream, or visualize, it is recommended that you clear the energy in your space first. In fact, it is good to make it a habit to do an energetic clearing of your space every day.

You may imagine a golden spiral of light that moves like a tornado and have it blow any stagnant energy up and out of the space.

You may want to clap your hands or ring Tibetan cymbals or any bells in every corner of your room.

You may light a candle, say a prayer or invocation, sing a song, or call in your guides and angels. Or do all of them. Do whatever feels right and natural for you.

Recycling the Collective Energy

As energy cannot be destroyed, let's set an intention to recycle it. The collective energy field is dense. If you are sensitive (and I'm supposing you are), it is important to make it a habit to clear your personal energetic space. You may do it with a simple intention statement.

If you would like put your hands out, palms up and imagine a big ball of light in your hands, and say out loud: *"I ask that any and all energy from this space that is not mine, nor for my highest good, come into this ball of light to be cleared, cleansed, and transmuted now."* Imagine the energy gathering in the ball and then send it up to the light, to the recycling center of the Universe.

A Meditation for Grounding and Connection

Grounding to the earth anchors you in the physical as you allow your consciousness to expand. Alignment and connection to the light of the Universe will enable you to be energized and infinitely supported. The power that creates universes flows through you.

As you read the following meditation, imagine the earth and the Universe at the same time, and feel the nurturing, cleansing energies as you journey with the words.

I recommend reading the words out loud, tasting, sensing, vibrating. See if it works for you.

Pause as you need.

Breathe in the energy of the earth. Feel as if you had roots through which you receive the nurturing and grounding energy of the earth. This energy supports you and receives you every step you take.

At the same time, imagine breathing in the gentle, soft light of the Universe through the crown of your head. Imagine, as a child would imagine, how this light activates every atom and photon in your energy system.

As you receive, you are received. Feel infinite love, acceptance, and blessing flowing through you.

Put one or both hands on your heart, allowing your heart to soften. See, feel, sense, and know how the energy of the earth and the light of the Universe are circulating through your heart, lighting up your whole being. Allow the energy to support, energize, harmonize, balance, lighten, and enlighten you, so that you remember who you are in truth: a beautiful, powerful child of the stars and the galaxies, free to fulfill your purpose.

You are free to choose the most magical and miraculous path for you.

You are infinitely supported.

You are accepted and valued. You are loved exactly as you are.

Instant Shift Tips

The fastest way to feel better is to make a conscious change in your body. In fact, knowing how your body language reflects energy and emotions will help you instantly shift your state of being.

Shift Your Body, Shift Your State of Being

Stand up for this so that your energy can flow freely, and you can stand tall.

Breathe deeply. Feel your feet on the ground. Stretch your body to warm up. Imagine standing confidently—feeling strong and balanced. Allow your body to reflect confidence to you. Your spine lengthens and back widens. Your chest expands and softens. Smile.

That's all. You are good to go.

If you would like, also experiment with the opposite to feel the difference: Collapse your body, look down, hunch your back, pull your face down. How does this feel? Make a whining sound.

Easy enough, choose consciously.

Instant Dopamine: Smile

Smiling releases dopamine, a feel-good hormone, in your body. Even if you fake your smile. It could not get simpler than this.

I remember fondly a barbershop quartet, a group of street performers who would sing on New York City subway cars, as we were traveling between stations. I saw them quite often when I was riding the number 1 train. Every time, they began: "Smile! It doesn't mess up your hair." And every time, they lit the whole subway car up.

Instant Clarity: Hydrate

After oxygen, water is the most essential life-sustaining element. Since our bodies and brains are 70–75 percent water, abundant hydration is of utmost importance. We need it to maintain the proper flow of our energy and healthy functioning of every system, organ, and cell in our physical bodies. Water's benefits include improved memory, concentration, reasoning, and emotional balance.

Whenever you are tired in the middle of the day, remind

yourself to enjoy a big glass of water. Aim to drink a glass of water approximately every hour or every two hours throughout the day. Even 2 percent dehydration affects our brain functions adversely.

Hold the glass of water between your hands, bless it, then drink it with gratitude.

Journal to Shift Your Story

Take a moment to begin exploring some questions for your journey to know yourself.

Look into all areas of your life: health, wellness, relationships, intuition, spirituality, money, finances, work, career, mission, purpose, emotions, growth, service, and contribution—or anything else that feels important to you.

Please reflect and write about each of the following aspects.

- Why are you reading this book? What do you wish to learn?
- Is there something you would like to change in your life?
- What are you ready to shift within the next three months? How will it change your life?
- What has to shift for you to be happy, free, and successful?
- Define the meaning of happiness, freedom, and success for yourself.

Your Wisdom Book

Begin writing in your wisdom book to fill it with insights so that in time it becomes a dependable source of inspiration for you.

- Think of a moment in your life when you were absolutely grateful. Finish the sentence and write in your wisdom book: *I am grateful for . . .*
  As you write, feel how it feels to be grateful.
- Look for a few quotes about gratitude for your wisdom book.
- Did you get a special insight while reading this chapter that you could write about in your wisdom book? Glance through the chapter again and look for a message that is relevant for you today.

TWO

WHAT IS A SIGN?

The Universe is talking to you. Are you listening?

W hether you believe in signs or care about them, you are receiving them, reading them, and interpreting them all the time, by default. We human beings operate our lives and organize information through signs and symbols, some of which belong to our collective stories and others to our personal narratives. While anything can be a sign, you give meaning to it based on your beliefs and values. You interpret and decode them based on your life experience and the story you tell yourself about reality. In fact, both your nervous system and the Universe create your version of reality based on your beliefs, values, and the dominant story you tell. Signs are part of an intricate web you weave through thought patterns, interpretations, feelings, and emotions.

The Universe reads the vibration of your energy and learns from you how to communicate with you. It meets you at the level of your frequency. Rewarding and fulfilling communication with the Universe requires knowing yourself and your individual way of understanding and making sense of the world. It requires being present in the now, understanding how energy works and learning to trust yourself and your intuition.

At its best, paying attention to signs can be a powerful way to stay in the flow of creation. Signs can help us make conscious choices and take inspired action with ease, grace, and flow.

To paraphrase the Nobel Prize-winning physicist Albert Einstein (1879–1955), we have a choice to live as though nothing is a miracle or as though everything is a miracle. The same goes for signs and synchronicities. We can live as though everything is a coincidence or as though nothing is a coincidence. It is your choice to give meaning to the events in your life.

The choice of story or interpretation we ascribe to events is important because everything that carries meaning directs our creative energy. The meaning we give to the now creates our future. Today will be tomorrow's yesterday. So, ask yourself this: What future memory are you creating at the moment?

Discover Your Sign Language

Every moment is a possibility for insight and awakening, for transformation and a new beginning. When you know yourself, you know your signs and vice versa.

Do you ever have the same dream over and over?

Do you notice that wherever you go, the same song is playing?

Are you seeing feathers or heart shapes?

Do rainbows appear? Or clouds with a form?

Do you repeatedly see symmetries, 13:31, 12:12, or double, triple, or quadruple digits, like 11, 22:11, 333, and 8888? Is any other number significant to you?

Perhaps you wake up at the same time every night.

While I will not give you answers to your signs' exact meaning, I am here to hold space for you to learn to trust your intuition and discover your own meaning. You might have your personal sign language that doesn't make any sense to anybody else. Well, it doesn't have to. It is between you and the Universe, between you and your consciousness. Tune in and pay attention to what hooks your interest. Often, the signs keep coming until you pay attention to them.

You might get the same message in many different ways. Signs might be something very familiar and show up in a way that makes perfect sense to you. But they also might be surprising, forcing you to stop and acknowledge them, even laugh out loud. Any reoccurring pattern can be a sign, a clue, or part of a puzzle. The Universe will use whatever it can to get your attention.

Your signs might be pointing the way to the future or

showing you something you need to know right now. The point of departure is always here and now, in the present moment.

This sounds obvious and simple, I know, but the mind can be sneaky. It will tell us stories to seduce us out of the present moment. When signs reflect our current story back to us, they can help us see where we are and make new choices. Signs can teach us to be present and flow with all that is so that there is more space to expand in the field of possibility so we may fulfill our dreams and visions.

Your signs are calling you to recognize your path and purpose. They point you to explore your innate gifts and talents, summoning you to your greatness. It is hard to recognize a sign if you ask for one in the middle of confusion, or if you are busy justifying, validating, projecting, explaining and filtering your signs through a disempowering story.

Your sign language is very personal to you. A sign can be a song, a poem, a word in a magazine cover, an overheard conversation, a phone call, a message. It can be anything that captures your curiosity. It is wonderful when a sign is a surprise and makes you attentive and aware. You'll know you received one if perhaps you think to yourself: *"This is exactly what I needed to hear or see"* or *"I never thought of that!"* When a sign surprises you, it might be easier for you to believe it is a sign. On the other hand, when you see a familiar sign, it can be very comforting. Perhaps a familiar sign confirms and lets you know that you are on track.

A sign can be a sound, such as a fire's crackling, a dog barking, or a car tooting its horn. Pay attention to timing and rhythm in your life. A sign can be an inner urge to do something, or a nudge to stop for a moment, or a hunch to take another route to your destination. A sign resides in what is important or meaningful to you. The signs speak your language. Your sign might not mean anything to someone else. It only needs to resonate with you.

A sign can be a picture, a photo, or a post on Facebook or Instagram. It can be a certain way the leaves have fallen on the ground. You might recognize a sign in ripples on water, a reflection in a window, or a shadow. It might hit you in a movie, an ad, or a jingle. Do you see how signs can be anything at all? Allow your imagination to lead the way. Be creative.

You might want to keep your journal next to your bed just in case. Dreams, as part of your Universe, speak your language. They communicate through images, symbols, sensations, feelings. Very rarely, a dream can be taken at face value. They are symbolic. They tell a story for you to interpret. You give them meaning.

In dreams, people seldomly represent themselves; instead, they represent an aspect of you or some other general aspect. Journaling about your dreams is a wonderful way to begin to understand how your intuitive language works. With both dreams and signs, and also life in general, someone can help you understand the process and hold space for you. Still, ultimately, only you can decipher and decide what anything means.

What if somehow every event and every sign were always revealing your purpose and leading you towards fulfillment?

You are free to choose to see any event as an opportunity rather than a problem. The more you use your imagination to find evidence of this kind of support, the greater your matrix of possibility becomes. I encourage you to be open to the possibility that signs are there to support you on your self-discovery and self-mastery.

What if everything in life was there *for* you and never against you?

You may choose it to be so, and so it is.

Are the Signs from the Universe?

Where do signs come from? Do they come from the Universe? You are the authority on your own signs. You know in your heart where your signs come from. They are part of your story. Trust yourself. Trust your signs. Trust your source. Your lexicon is between you and the Universe.

While you are the ultimate ruler in your realm and get to decide where your signs come from (and which ones even qualify as signs), it is beneficial to let go of any preconceived ideas of what a sign should be. Look around and see the world with the eyes of curiosity. Play with childlike wonder and discover the magic and miracle in everything. Close your eyes and imagine feeling the salt of the ocean in the air on the beach. Allow the wind to caress your face. Listen to the sound of the rain and ride the rainbows. Hear the flow of life in your veins. Life is calling you. Your soul is beckoning you, *"Come, this is the way."*

Signs work very much like a GPS system. As you flow, shift, and transform, the matrix of possibility changes—and so do your signs. Your starting point is always now, and your destination is always where you are going *now.* An absolute final destination doesn't exist in your GPS, nor does it care where you were yesterday. The same is true for the signs of the Universe. A sign indicates where you are or points in the direction you are going. But it doesn't necessarily indicate any destination further than that, nor where you end up all together. Signs light the way and confirm your path.

Are events in our lives predestined?

The way I see it at the moment is that we are born with a unique matrix of possibility. I imagine it as a luminous, multidimensional web of sacred geometry. At any given time in space, we are operating within a field of possibility in our matrix. But the matrix shifts as we shift. When we make a choice, conscious or not, our whole matrix changes and the operational field of possibility with it. So, to answer the above question: each choice either contracts or expands the matrix. Each intricate field within the matrix has its own "destiny" and internal consequences. But the moment we shift again, the field rearranges itself, and so does our destiny.

As the vibrational signal we give out becomes clearer and more elevated, our matrix expands. We are then supported by higher levels of consciousness. The infinite potentiality of the Universe is always supporting us, but we are met at the level of our vibration. When we expand, the Universe expands.

How to Ask for a Sign

Ask, and you shall receive. This is true. The clearer you are when you ask, the clearer an answer you'll receive. And the more detached you are from the outcome, the easier your answer comes. Begin teaching yourself to elevate your state, your vibration first, before having a conversation with the Universe, or asking it for a sign. This way, you can free yourself to receive an answer from a clearer perspective. Make a ritual to clear your space. Ground and center yourself. Perhaps light a candle or say a prayer. Or go to a place in nature where you may feel more grounded and feel free to speak your request out loud.

When you want or need a sign, keep the request simple. Ask directly. I always ask out loud. If you prefer, write your request down. You may want to write a letter to the Universe. This can help clarify your intention.

Get into the habit of using your voice. Sound carries the

energy of your intention powerfully. It makes sense to use vibration to communicate with a vibrational Universe. By using your voice, you are vibrationally summoning the essence and energy of your request. You are making a clear commitment through your voice, signaling to your brain to prioritize and go find the sign.

In fact, when you state anything clearly, it is so. It will show up in one form or another unless there is a contradictory vibration active somewhere in your system.

Begin by asking for information about something simple. Play with the Universe so that you may learn to trust your knowing with ease and lightness, rather than pushing through frustration, nervousness, or worry.

Be honest with yourself. Instead of being invested in the answer or trying to fool yourself by asking for a sign you desperately want, detach yourself from the outcome. Ground yourself, feel the support of the Universe, set an intention for clarity and truth. Then allow the sign to be revealed to you.

Leave room for it to be a surprise.

Signs of Confirmation

We often feel the need for reassurance or a validation of what we already know or confirmation of a sign we already received but are doubting. It is very human to doubt, but it is also possible to learn to trust yourself and the information you perceive. When you trust yourself, all signs serve more or less as a confirmation. Even so, always filter any signs through your heart and your inner Truth-o-Meter.

When in doubt, pause and ask for clarification. If necessary, wait for another sign. Never go against your gut feeling. It is probably safe to say that we all have gone against our gut feeling at one point or another. Just the other day, I clearly heard in my head, *The coffee cup is too close to the edge of the table.* I chose to leave the coffee there anyway, and sure enough, the next moment, it fell.

When working with clients—whether in person or at a distance—I do my best to ensure that my personality doesn't interfere with the healing work. I imagine Ulla, the Diva, going out to have her double espresso, and Ulla, the Wise Woman, staying to attend the client. A while back, I was doing a healing session for a client in New York City. I had my physical eyes closed and felt at peace. Through my inner eye, I "saw" a beautiful female form wearing a light blue gown and a long translucent veil. The veil did not cover her luminous face, yet as she was the pure essence of beauty, light, and love, I couldn't make out the details. Her arms were by her sides, palms facing me as if blessing. Her communication was through my heart. She "told" me she was Mother Mary and that she supports all healing and ascension work through the light of her compassionate heart as her gift to humankind. She communicated very clearly to me: *"No matter what, you are loved and supported.*

Always." It was like osmosis, direct transmission through her vibration to every atom of my being. I didn't have to understand it intellectually. My figuring-out mind stood still for a moment. Just witnessing.

I have no way of telling you what really happened, or if it actually happened. I have no need to prove that it really was Mother Mary. It felt very real, albeit in a dreamlike way. I felt totally blessed. Something shifted in my heart. I was left resonating with an inexplicable feeling of truth of an enigmatic encounter.

The following day, still sensing the beautiful vision's deep peace, I was wearing another one of my many hats. I had a gig as a musician with a trio consisting of flute, violin, and cello. We were to provide elegant background music for a dinner party. Armed with my flute, wearing all black, I was on my way to Long Island with scores of Mozart, Haydn, Bach, Telemann, Vivaldi, and other favorites in my backpack.

My colleagues and I did this kind of work all the time. As a group leader, I always made sure to book the best people for these background jobs so that we could have a great time playing together. Because we had all performed at Lincoln Center and other prestigious concert venues around the world, we would set the bar high and show up to these gigs with concert quality. Still, there is no such thing as "just" a gig in my book or no "just" anything to this day. You don't switch yourself on and off. It is a choice I live by. Always show up genuinely, offering your absolute best.

As we arrived at the dinner venue, I saw a good-sized group of monks mixing among the other dinner guests. What was peculiar to me was that they were wearing simple light blue robes. I had only seen brown ones before. I asked what the event was and why the blue robes.

"Oh, we are celebrating the rite of ordination in the Brotherhood of Mary. Light blue is Mother Mary's color."

Hmm. Interesting.

We started playing. The place had nice acoustics and we had fun making music.

When we paused for a break, my colleagues went to eat. As I was still putting my flute away, one of the monks came to me. He said, *"Thank you so much for the music. It makes such a difference not only in this space but in the world. I would love to give you a gift of appreciation, but I don't own much of anything as a monk. Would you accept this medallion of Mary as my gift? This was first made to commemorate Mary's apparition to someone in the eighteen-hundreds. This medallion is often called the Miraculous Medal and was originally made to bring blessings to anyone who wears it."*

I didn't know at the time how to tell him about my vision of Mary the previous night without feeling disrespectful. I received his gift with great gratitude and tears of happiness. While he will never know the depth of the meaning his gift had for me, I think he knew from my reaction that this meant much more to me than an ordinary thank-you-for-the-music gift.

We Are Signs for Each Other

Your smile can make a difference. Your message to someone can arrive precisely at the right time. Your social media post can give even a stranger a piece of a puzzle they need. One of those moments when you say, *"This is exactly what I needed."*

The more you show up aligned and authentic, the more your presence can guide others. The more you see meaning in everything, the more the Universe can use you as a sign for someone else.

A few years ago, after I had done a small presentation of music and stories at a major university, I received an email from one of the students there. She had been on campus that day when she heard the sound of my flute all of a sudden. She knew she was to follow the sound. She began to move in the flute's direction, stopping when the sound stopped and moving towards it when it started again. Finally, she arrived at the space of my presentation. She stayed and listened. Something shifted in her. The sound of my flute hooked her attention that day, that moment. Something in my performance shifted her energy and intention. She explained in her letter that she had been on her way to kill herself.

I personally choose to believe that I was placed there for

her. It feels too big a deal to be a coincidence. For sure, I wasn't there trying to save anyone. I was there doing what I love, playing my small part in the big scheme of life.

The young woman might not ever have written to me, and if she hadn't, I wouldn't have known. Perhaps she wrote to me to be my sign, and now she is yours. You might not see the impact you have in the world. It is not the point to make an impact. The point is to show up with honesty, integrity, and vulnerability, exactly as you are. Trust the humanity and the immensity within you. The same energy that creates worlds flows through you.

You are infinitely supported.

Infinitely loved.

Exactly as you are.

Make a Vision Board

Because the human brain works well with visual representation, a beautiful, inspiring, and efficient way to engage with the energy of your dreams and visions is to create a good-old vision board. While digital boards available on the internet would work perfectly well for this purpose, I personally love to have the tactile experience of making a collage on paper. This arts and crafts experience engages various aspects of my creativity.

Feel free to choose which one, the digital or the paper, resonates with you. Or neither.

Choose the size of the board that feels right and makes

sense for your space. If only a certain-sized paper is available and you would like to make a larger board, then tape together smaller pieces of paper to create the bigger canvas for your dreams.

If you want to write on the board, have colored markers or pens available.

Then, all you need are scissors, glue, and a pile of old magazines. Start cutting out photos and words representing the essence of your ideal life or what you intend to manifest. You can also print out pictures and/or words from the internet or your computer.

The simple act of looking for pictures and power words will program your brain, train your imagination, and entrain the Universe to look for them, recognize them, and bring them to you. Feel your excitement and fill your heart with gratitude every time you work on your board or look at it.

Imagine. How would it feel to live the new story of your life? How would it feel to have it all? Feel it as if it were all yours now. The synchronicities will begin to kick in to match the joy of your vision and the vibration of your gratitude. Note that while you ask: *How would it feel to live my dream life?* Allow the answer to come in a "present tense" feeling of it. Even when you journal about this, you don't answer "it *would* feel . . . ," instead, feel it in the now, as if it was truly happening. That way, it elevates and inspires, and changes your chemistry to reprogram your reality.

Making a vision board is a beautiful way to explore the essence of your dreams, purpose, gifts, talents, value, and meaning, and a powerful way to deliver the memo to the Universe.

As you fill the board with pictures, words, and colors that symbolize the heart and the feeling of what you are manifesting, these all become part of your energy field and vibration, the lexicon of your new story, and the mental programming for your new life. You will almost certainly begin to see signs that you recognize as signs from the vision on your board. So many extraordinary stories of people who have manifested exactly what is on their boards time and time again.

Everything is first created vibrationally, as an idea, thought, vision, or a dream. Your feeling moves it through time and space until it is 99.99 percent fully in place vibrationally before you ever see a sign of it in the physical dimension. Trust your vision. Stay with it. Commit to it. What can stop the flow of its manifestation is fear and doubt. Give it your highest attention and the most joyous focus. Say to yourself: *This, or something better, now manifests in my life.*

Once I put a picture of a dolphin on my vision board. I loved the essence of the dolphin, the playful, joyous, fluid energy it represented for me. I didn't think too much of it. A few days later, two ladies from Hawaii wrote to me, saying they would be in Cusco for only one day and would like to meet me. They had followed a sign to find my contact info because someone in Lima had mentioned my name—only my first name—and that I lived in Cusco. These resourceful ladies, armed only with my first name and the fact that I play the flute, found me on the internet.

This was divine timing because I had just gotten home that day from a trip, and they would leave the following day. We met over a vegetarian wood-fired pizza and felt an immediate easy-flow soul connection. A few short months later, I was in Hawaii swimming with dolphins together with these two amazing wise women.

Mind you, Hawaii had not been on my board, nor was it on my list specifically. Still, it was brought to me because of the essence of the dolphin, the messenger. I wouldn't have known to ask for Hawaii specifically. Yet, the journey to Hawaii turned out to be one of the most important ones I've ever taken in my life so far because I ended up finding a very important piece of myself through that journey. This experience showed me the importance of listening to the nudges and whispers of inspiration without knowing where they lead you.

Pay attention to the essence of encounters with strangers, messages, conversations, words, images, colors, numbers, and sounds.

PLAY WITH THE UNIVERSE

Imagination is a tool for your intuition. It is your best friend in creation and in seeing the signs everywhere. Let's begin imagining and expanding in the field of possibility.

A Meditation to Receive a Sign from the Universe

Think of a question for which you would like to ask for a sign or an area of your life for which you would like guidance or clarification. Let's go on a journey to see what you are shown. Read the following meditation, "Receive a Sign from the Universe," slowly, with rich imagination. Pause as you need. Honor your way of imagining. Sense, see, feel, listen.

You may also listen to it as a guided meditation on my website or YouTube channel (see Resources for details).

Allow a deep, loving breath through your nose, inhaling slowly. Exhale through your mouth. Feel how your whole body is filling with warm golden light. Your body is relaxing, deeply relaxing, as you continue breathing.

Right now, there is nothing to do, nothing to figure out.

34

Just be here now.

Just be.

Imagine that you are walking on a beautiful, magical path. It is your path of guidance . . . and clarity . . .and peace . . . and harmony . . . and love. This is a path of light and higher guidance, and only the energy of the highest light can enter here. It feels safe.

Feel the warmth of the sun caressing your body. Perhaps there is a gentle breeze on your face. Feel how, with each step you take, the energy of the earth receives you, nurtures you, supports you. Inhale the fragrance of the earth.

As you walk along the winding path, you see a luminous temple at the top of a small hill. You begin making your way up the hill towards the temple.

Look around you.

What do you see?

You might see crystals, flowers, animals, trees, angels, fairies, feathers, rainbows of all colors, or anything that has meaning for you.

Allow what you see to be what you need to see right now.

Imagination is a tool for your intuition. There is no limit to your imagination.

Remind yourself of your infinite connection to source energy and listen to your heart and intuition and guidance.

Follow your heart and intuition and guidance.

Listen, feel, sense, and know.

Allow each unfolding moment to reveal its gifts, its information, its signs.

Be present in the now—with all your senses. This is a new moment, a new opportunity to see, to feel, to create, and to receive.

As you walk up the hill, easily and effortlessly, as if you were floating, your vibration is elevated. As you go higher, your frequency shifts ever so slightly higher, and higher. You feel lighter and lighter.

Now you come to your temple of light. Notice any details.

What shape is the temple? What color?

What material is it made of?

How do you enter?

Are there stairs?

What kind of doorway is there?

Are there any details on the door? Symbols? Numbers? What color is it? How do you open it?

Or is it already open?

Don't think. Imagine as a child would imagine.

Enter the temple. What do you see?

Feel the light. Observe the dance of the light in the air. Allow the sacredness of this moment to transform you.

Find a place that feels right for you to sit down. And just bathe for a moment in the gentle energy of your temple. Allow your cells to be rejuvenated. Allow the space between your cells to be energized.

Imagine a soft sphere of light within your heart. Feel your heart softening. And softening a little more.

Imagine how the soft light begins to expand in your heart. It expands and expands so that it overflows and soon surrounds you and fills the entire temple, then expands beyond the temple so that you truly feel connected with all that is, was, and will be through this light—your light.

Listen to your heart, dear one.

You are a magnificent being of the light, a child of the sun and the moon, the stars and the galaxies. You are love, you are light, you are one with the Universe.

Feel the pulsation in your heart, saying: "I love you. I love you. I love you. Thank you."

As you raise your vibration, your matrix of possibilities changes. You can elevate yourself to be ready to trust life, trust yourself, and trust your signs.

Trust the source of all that is, as you understand it.

You are an important and unique expression of that consciousness.

You are never alone.

Trust.

Now imagine a door opening slowly to your temple. Watch as in comes a messenger. You may imagine him, her, or it in any form that pleases you. Is your messenger a woman? A man? An animal? Light?

The messenger gives you a box and then bids you farewell. Thank your messenger silently.

What color is the box?

How big is it?

What material is it made of?

Is there anything written on it?

Remember, you asked for a sign at the beginning of our journey. There was a question or need for clarity or guidance in some area of your life.

Open the box. Again, don't think. Allow the box to reveal to you anything at all that only you would know how to interpret.

This is your sign. And you know what it means.

You can come to this temple at any time. But now it is time to thank the temple and to thank yourself.

Now, go out the door and back down the path.

Pay attention to the path. Has it changed?

Whatever you need, receive it from your path now.

Feel the light and lightness of your path. See the signs everywhere. Trust yourself. Trust life. Trust your path. The truth is that you are way greater than you *ever thought possible. The earth and the heavens support you. Always. The energy that creates worlds flows through you. You are it. It is you.*

When you are ready, wiggle your fingers and stretch your body. Allow a deep, loving breath. With your breath, own your body, own your life, and own this moment fully and completely.

Journal to Shift Your Story

Studies show that journaling or taking notes by hand uses larger parts of your brain than typing. Handwriting reaches areas of brain equal to meditation, allowing you to process language, learning, healing and memory in a way that doesn't happen if you type. Writing by hand allows you to slow down, which is good to dream up your new life. Due to the increased neural activity your imagination and your creative juices flow more generously when handwriting.

Receive a Sign from the Universe

Whenever you journal after any event or meditation, allow your own wisdom and intuition expand not only on the experience, but also on what you need to know at this time. Instead of only remembering the details, allow further insight and information to flow through you when you write.

Consider the many moments and possibilities that were

there in the meditation for you to receive guidance and signs.

- What was the most important part of the meditation journey for you today?
- What did you see, hear, feel? How was the path? What were you wearing?
- What did the temple look like outside? Inside? Was the door open?
- What does all that mean to you? There is no right or wrong answer. Only your interpretation. Imagine like a child would imagine.
- Who was the messenger?
- What was the box like? What was in the box?
- What does it mean to you?

You may listen to this meditation again at any time and allow the sign or signs to be different. It is designed to provide you with answers based on what you need at any given moment.

Your Lexicon of Signs

Start making a list of possible signs for you. Anything that hooks your attention. Be general at first: symbols, pictures, songs, colors, shivers, tingles, animals, nature elements, words, numbers, sounds.

You may add to your list at any time.

For you to recognize something as a sign, it has to have some importance to you on some level. If you say: *"Might this be a sign?"* Add it to your list. Which ones are your favorite signs? Or your power signs?

The Meaning of Your Signs

Pick a sign from your lexicon. Explore some questions. Trust your answers. Do this with as many signs you would like. You become better and better in getting answers once you get started.

- What in this sign hooks your attention?
- How does it make you feel?
- Does it appear repeatedly, or only once?
- Does it confirm or inform?
- If you described it with one word, what would it be?
- Does it answer a question or point a direction?
- Is it reflective or fun? Does it inspire or empower?
- If it was a color, what color would it be?
- If it was a feeling, what feeling would it be?
- What does it mean to you?

Synchronicities and Signs

Journal about synchronicities and signs in your life, past and present. We all have such stories of encounters, song lyrics, conversations, videos, pictures, posts, or overheard conversations, even miraculous and magical moments, those that you say: *"This really happened to me."*

There are no limits: imagine, dream, play.

Write it all down. Tell a story.

41

Your Wisdom Book

Your wisdom book is yours. You choose what goes in.

- Keep filling it with quotes, poems, and insights you see or hear and like. You may search the internet for quotes. Try different keywords that ignite your curiosity, for example: possibility, miracles, synchronicity, intuition, signs, symbols.

- As gratitude is one of the most potent ways to elevate your vibration and become a magnet for blessings, make it a daily habit to write at least three reasons to be grateful in your wisdom book: *I am grateful for* ...

- What was the most important message for you in this chapter? I ask this, so that you begin making it a habit to pay attention. Write it into your wisdom book either in your own words or mine.

Instant Shift Tips

Here are two simple yet effective physical techniques for interrupting a pattern and resetting your energy system.

You can shift your state of being in an instant by changing your body and posture. Learn what works for you and invent more ways to stop a limiting thought from going any further.

Choose your favorite ones and use them often.

You will find all the instant shift tips demonstrated on my website (see Resources for details).

Instant Energy Flow

Stand straight, feet about shoulder-width apart. Place your weight on the balls of your feet and begin light, gentle bouncing on your heels. As you bounce, allow your whole body to shake softly, keeping your arms, wrists, shoulders, and joints loose. Do this light shake for 20–30 seconds, then slowly slow down and come back to stillness. This great reset allows your life force energy to flow freely, releases stress from your body, and practically activates and regenerates all your vital systems.

Instant Reset

A short shake of your whole body while allowing a sound with your cheeks flapping loosely. Do this to reset and to intentionally interrupt unwanted thoughts and patterns. Let go of anything and everything that doesn't serve you at this time.

You might have seen this described in my TEDx Talk, "Do You See the Signs of the Universe?"

THREE

TUNE YOURSELF AS AN INSTRUMENT

You are a flute through which the infinite longs to make music.

How do you know if the Universe is talking to you? How do you make sense of signs? You not only *have* your own factory-installed GPS system, but you *are* it. More poetically, you are a flute through which the infinite makes music. You are music sounding and resounding in the Universe. You are both the music and the instrument.

Regardless of circumstances you can choose to shift, pivot, center, balance, and flow with peace and freedom in the midst of any turmoil. To say we live in an unprecedented time of change and transformation is an understatement. Our technology creates constant information overload for the mind and the senses, which is why it is easy to get confused and overwhelmed. We yearn for clarity in the middle of confusion. If we wait for the outside to change, we feel out of control, but we can learn to shift our inner state and reclaim our power. Did you know that there is a part of your brain that filters all the sensorial data entering your system? A part that can be programmed to transform your experience and perception of reality?

The Reticular Activating System

There is a little pinky-sized part of your brain called the reticular activating system, or RAS, that works as a guardian or a bouncer for the brain, filtering all the information from your sensorial system, with one exception. Interestingly, smells go straight to the emotional centers of your brain. The RAS is a small detail very much worth knowing, because its function directly affects your ability to take responsibility of your life, to shift your story, and to see signs that truly are helpful.

As a whole, the sensorial system transmits roughly 11 million bits per second of data to your brain. Your bouncer, the RAS, determines which ones are allowed through the door by assessing what is and what is not relevant information for you. How does it do this? It bases the information content on your repetitive thoughts, habits, beliefs, opinions, and values. In other words, it validates your story by allowing you to see only what you instruct it to see. It works on your command. It finds proof for your story.

Your RAS also filters your signs to show you only pertinent ones based on your dominant story and the energetic vibration you offer.

According to all the data gathered and filtered, the neurons fire and wire to build intricate neuronal pathways in your brain. The sophisticated biochemistry alchemizes the information into your physical reality. Neurological studies show conclusively that the brain doesn't differentiate between what is real and what is imagined. It fires the neurons the same way for an imaginary event as it does for something that is actually happening. This is powerful information. Use it.

It is important to take command of your power, so that you don't become a victim of your own story—so that you can choose more consciously with what to program your brain and the Universe. The program consists of thoughts you offer and the vibrational essence of your feelings and emotions. This is the key to optimize your energy system, to direct your story, and to support the miracle you are. This connection between your thoughts and feelings, your brain, body and the Universe is the key to all healing, manifesting, transformation and creation.

When you learn to focus your thoughts and emotions greater than doubts, fears, and other limitations, you raise your vibration, which then signals the Universe to allow consciousness to move through on a new, higher level and in a miraculous way.

To be creation in action, it is vital to first tune the instrument that you are so the highest consciousness of the Universe may flow through you and create as you.

Be Present: Embody the Infinite Now

Only in the present moment do we have any power. I am often asked how to stay present, or how to hold on to a good-feeling vibe or a state of peace or clarity. There isn't any holding on. Change is our natural state of being. The now-moment we experience is like a flowing river or a wave rippling across the surface of the ocean. We don't hold on to it, we surrender to it and learn to ride the wave.

Imagine surfing a big wave on a board. There is nothing to hold on to and you can't look back. To stay on your feet and ride the wave successfully, you must stay focused and balance yourself. The more you practice, the more you learn to trust yourself. The easier it is to hold your balance.

Learning to read your intuition from moment to moment is like that. Life is also like that, except as we learn to surf the wave, we *become* the wave.

The only way to access the space of creation and become one with the field of possibility is to embrace infinity and be present, to flow in the now. You always have a choice in the now. A choice to shift your reality. A choice to transform your point of creation. You can change any part of your story now. Choose to be present and embody the infinite now.

When you are present, you are both still and in motion simultaneously. There is livingness in that stillness. When you learn to center yourself in that living stillness, you enter a space of clarity, where you can know the truth of your being, where the signs and answers are clear, transparent and coherent. Through clarity and authentic presence, it is easy for you to take inspired action and become an instrument and a container for a new and expanded vision yourself in the space of creation.

Finetuning Your Senses

Your senses help you make sense of the world. Your brain processes sensorial information, interpreting it as something you can understand and accept. When you become conscious of your ability to shift your state of being and thus to change the way your brain interprets information, you truly can become free of the limitations that keep you from fulfilling your path and purpose. Awakening your senses and playing with the Universe consciously not only will enrich your everyday experience, but it will also activate your extrasensory skills, finetune your vibrational perception and enhance your intuition.

Each of your physical senses is a gateway to the secrets of the Universe.

We so easily take our bodies for granted, and by doing so, dismiss our capacity to perceive the invisible, inaudible, subtler frequencies of our existence. Being fully present in the physical body allows us to expand in consciousness to being present with the Universe. The body is a sacred temple. To allow a full human experience in which the spirit soars completely free while embodied, we need to consciously acknowledge, honor, and enjoy the fabulous body temple. As you already know, when you shift your physiology, you instantly shift how you feel.

Your body can limit you or set you free.

I invite you to play with your senses, to feel into the world around you consciously, so that you may begin to trust your own knowing and guidance here and now, and expand all the way into the higher consciousness of all that is, was and will be.

You See Better with Your Eyes Closed

I once was teaching an improvisation class to a group of six- and seven-year-old beginner musicians. It was a small group consisting of violinists, pianists and flutists. Most of them knew how to play only a couple of notes on their instruments. Our class took place at a summer camp in the middle of nature. We made musical stories by interpreting everything around us through sound: feelings, colors, animals, wind, sun, sky, questions, answers. We played with the idea of listening with all our being and imagining stories that we then would perform with sound and movement only.

One morning, the little ones were sitting on the floor in a circle, and I asked them to close their eyes. I began telling a story. I asked them to listen to the sounds around them, which then became part of our miraculous story in a magical forest. After a moment of everyone squeezing their eyes closed and imagining intently, one girl swung her eyes wide open and declared with all her innocent excitement:

"Oooh, with your eyes closed you see soooo much better!"

In her breakthrough insight, she discovered a deep truth about "seeing" with the inner eye, about engaging her imagination as a tool for creativity and intuition.

The physical sight is the most dominant one of the senses and it tends to take over in terms of what information is delivered to our brain. Closing the eyes heightens the other senses. Out of all the 11 million bits per second of sensorial data, about 10 million bits per second come through our eyes alone. Only about fifty bits get through to the brain altogether. This is why I do most of my private distant coaching sessions on audio only, to save the bandwidth for feeling and sensing, rather than looking at the screen. Let's make the fifty bits out of 11 million count.

To practice "inner" seeing with your eyes open, begin looking at different things without defining or naming anything. Let go of any story or explanation. Just breathe and feel the intimacy of the gentle interaction taking place. Relax and expand into beingness, into seeing, allowing, connecting. Your eyes resting.

Be present with whatever you are looking at, as if there were a secret just between the two of you. If a story shows up, gently pause, breathe, and focus in your unbiased way of seeing again. Make friends with colors, shapes, dimensions, light, and shadow. See everything as if for the first time. Be in awe like a child would be, still with no story. As if you didn't know the names of anything.

Everything is new and unique.

Imagine seeing with the eyes of love.

If you can, go for a walk, ideally in a park, a forest, a beach, and allow the same kind of intimacy with trees, plants, flowers, stones, and water. If you can, kick off your shoes and go barefoot. Awaken your ability to receive from the invisible web of information of all livingness. If for any reason you cannot go out for a walk or have no access to nature, then use your imagination.

Take a moment to close your eyes and imagine yourself in nature. Feel the ground, the wind, the birdsong in your heart. Imagine travelling to faraway places and allow the energy of the place to inspire, heal and support you. I love visiting some of my favorite power places in my imagination, in meditation or dream time. Or you may also enjoy my other favorite travel destination: the stars and the galaxies.

Pay Attention

We often miss the sunset or the moonrise because we are busy describing it or taking a picture of it for our social media. Don't get me wrong, I love seeing the world through the lens of my camera and I enjoy going for meditative walks with my camera. As it captures light that's invisible to the human eye, it feels like it is teaching me, expanding me. My camera is an extension of my intuition in a similar way my flute is. Where my camera shows me how to see, my flute shows me how to listen. Learn to discern, however, when taking a photo distracts you from being present and when it brings you to the infinite now with its gifts and possibilities.

Once in Peru, when I was leading a sacred journey for someone, we received a powerful sign at the summit of Machu Picchu mountain, an ancient ceremony site high above the famous Inca sanctuary, the archeological site. I had just finished a guided meditation on the union of the sacred feminine and the sacred masculine, when, right there in front of us, just a few feet from the precipice, a condor couple appeared suddenly, soaring together. The female was very close, I could have hopped on her back, her huge wings almost moving the air on my face. The male was a little farther away. For a split second, I thought of grabbing my camera. Quickly, I let the thought go and surrendered to be in the majestic presence of these powerful living symbols of the Andes. Had I reached for my camera I would have missed the moment. I will forever treasure this breathtaking experience and blessing as a powerful sign and a sacred gift from Machu Picchu and the Andes.

Some tourists a few feet away from us were taking selfies and didn't even see the condors. When we were ready to begin descending from the mountain, I asked the old guardian who was on duty that day, if he had seen the condors. He smiled with his teeth green from coca leaves and said: *"Oh, yes. They came only for you, señorita."*

Just to be clear, it is quite rare to see condors in Machu Picchu these days. I told a friend down in the pueblo, and he couldn't believe it, saying, *"I have lived here for thirty years and never seen a single condor."*

Listen with Your Whole Being

Close your eyes and listen. Listen with your skin, your breath, your nose, your eyes, your toes, your eyelashes. Listen with your whole being. Be aware of the sounds and rhythms within and around you. Listening goes deeper than just merely perceiving sound. When you become the listening space, you recognize your signs in words and whispers, in sounds and shivers.

When I was twenty years old, I was rehearsing the Poulenc and Prokofiev flute sonatas with a wonderful pianist in Rome, Italy. He was blind and had learned his part from reading braille scores. We rehearsed at his apartment, where it was quite dark for obvious reasons. I observed how he listened, how he caressed every note like a treasure. I found myself closing my eyes frequently when playing with him. There, in that dark room in Rome, was one of my awakening moments. It shifted my listening in a magical way, not just for music, but for life.

One day my Italian colleague wanted to show me *"the most beautiful piazza you will ever see."* His words. We walked for a good while. He knew his way. He would warn me of steps and such. He listened to his surroundings. He could hear a bike approaching. When we arrived at the piazza, he was beaming. *"Isn't this the most beautiful piazza in the world?"* As we sat on a bench, I closed my eyes and the dimensions of its beauty started to be revealed. There was the music of the water fountain, not just the main *whoosh,* but the sound of the droplets around it. The gentle fragrance of the roses, as if they were letting me in on a secret. All of a sudden, tranquil church bells joined the rhythm of someone sweeping the street. The aroma of freshly ground coffee beans blended with an occasional friendly *"Ciao"* with short, melodious chat echoing there in the most beautiful piazza of the world. Just like the little girl in the magical, miraculous forest, I felt that with my eyes closed I could see so much better.

The Power of Gratitude

You probably know that gratitude is important. Are you actively using this knowledge? If you are, you know how life-changing it is. If you kind-of-sort-of are, commit to it fully for three months and see what happens. Gratitude is perhaps *the* most powerful healer and activator around. When you begin to focus your energy of gratitude with crystalline clarity and unwavering attention to not only all that you already are or have, but to everything your heart desires, you prep and prime your life for a miraculous expansion. Make a commitment to see what happens when you fill your life with the feeling and vibration of gratitude.

Neurological studies have shown that gratitude is one of the most potent ways to free neurotransmitters dopamine and serotonin in our system, resulting in a verifiable change in brain chemistry in terms of overall wellness and energy. Your neurochemical intelligence responds to the feeling and frequency of it.

Gratitude prepares you to receive. Imagine holding, having, and being the essence of what you are manifesting with a deep sense of gratitude, as if it already were your fabulous reality, and—*ta-dah!*—your brain begins scanning your environment looking for all the possible ways for you to receive it. Being in a state of gratitude makes you a container for receiving and at the same time strengthens all your physical systems, including your immune system.

Let's use our superpower called *"Thank you."* But rather than just listing things and counting your blessings, embrace and welcome gratitude as a state of being, and preferably a permanent state of being. Create a habit of seeing your life through the eyes of appreciation.

Appreciate all parts of your body. Be conscious of the miracle you are. Say, *"Thank you, skin. Thank you, eyes. Thank you, mouth. Thank you, arms.* And also, *"Thank you heart, kidneys, liver, lungs, blood."* Feel gratitude for your perfect radiant health in every cell of your body.

Feel gratitude for everything around you, such as your home, your bed, your bathroom, the sky, the wind, the earth, flowers, your breath, food, water, colors, textures, animals, people, poetry, and music. Stop for a moment and acknowledge the abundance around you. It is always there in one form or another. When you appreciate everything, more will come to you. Appreciation is a gateway to receiving.

Begin imagining the essence of your ideal life, and as a result extending gratitude to your future. Really feel the gratitude in every atom of your being, as if you were living your dream life now. Feel the joy of it, and see it, hear it, smell it, touch it, taste it. How would it feel to live it fully? This is the way you program it into your brain and then the Universe says yes.

Be grateful for harmony and balance within your mind and spirit. Feel the essence of love permeating every area of your life in splendid, surprising ways. Allow a deep feeling of purpose and fulfillment now. Invoke the feeling of living your dream life now, as real as you possibly can. Choose it. Love it. Embody it.

You can accelerate and magnify manifestation and transformation by giving thanks for it now, by appreciating every aspect of it in your imagination now. Remember, your brain and creation system takes everything you feed it at face value; it doesn't differentiate between a past story of resentment and your most powerful, highest version of yourself you can imagine.

Your brain takes your feeling as a guide to go to work, to create a perfect match for it in the physical.

Anchor Reminders Through Your Senses

Choose a couple of things you do every day and assign them to be mini-meditations, rituals, announcements to the Universe, brief moments where you pause and remind yourself gently to be present, to breathe, to be grateful, to shift your vibration. Use your senses for this. In the morning, when you have your juice, coffee, tea, or a glass of water, whatever your morning drink is, hold it in your hands for a moment. Allow this moment to remind you to stand tall, to breathe deeply and choose your state of being.

Bless your drink with an intention for whatever you need at the moment, be it healing, clarity, energy, peace, anything. When you bless it with an intention, if possible, say it out loud. Include gratitude in it. Say something such as: *"Thank you for being my elixir of joy today."* Smile.

When you shower or wash yourself, do a cleansing and gratitude ritual. Wash every part of your beautiful, miraculous body with appreciation. Be gentle, as if you were washing a child. Give extra love to any part of your body that might be hurting or in pain. The skin sends a million bits of information per second to our brain through the RAS filter.

It can be frustrating if we are sick or in pain. As we want to get rid of the pain, we might reject the hurting parts. We push against the pain and just want it to be over. What if you allowed a gentle space for healing instead, and began cheering your body's innate ability to heal itself? Use the moments in the shower to program loving, accepting, honoring, and valuing data into your system. Choose to be on your own side.

Take time to eat. Thank your food. Set the table nicely even if it is just for yourself. When you bite an apple, feel its texture. Make eating the apple your reminder to be present here and now.

Remember, the sense of smell goes directly to your brain's emotional centers. Explore the scents around you, flowers, spices, herbs, oils, incense, foods. Enjoy the pleasures of the fragrances and discover which ones calm you, uplift you, inspire you, energize you. Take an aromatic bath and make it a celebration of your senses. If you don't have a bathtub, soak your feet in a bucket or pail with a drop of your favorite bath oil in it.

Throughout your day, take breaks, even if it is for three minutes, to connect with your body in space. Stretch. Dance. Choose music that literally moves you and allows your body to express itself freely. Make a playlist for yourself for each different energy and intention.

Shake off limitations.

Dance as a wild person, dance as consciousness, dance as power, dance as luminosity. Dance as choice and commitment. Caress the Universe with your dance. Allow your molecules to dance with you and to rearrange themselves into a renewed, fabulous you.

Hug yourself. Pat yourself on the back. Tell yourself what an outstanding job you're doing. Praise yourself. Tell yourself: *"You are amazing. I am so proud of you."* Or anything else you would like to hear.

Even going to the bathroom can be a ritual, a release ritual, *"I now release the old and all that doesn't serve me. Thank you, thank you, thank you."*

Design ordinary moments as anchors to remind you to

be present throughout your day. Remind yourself that you have a choice. Any action you repeat from day to day can function as your own unique ritual. Use your imagination to create new ones.

These simple everyday mini-rituals can help program and condition you to your point of power. They don't take any extra time, yet by consciously choosing to be present with them you will begin feeling more alive and energized in your body and perhaps noticing how small things in life can make a big difference in your overall mood and energy.

Playing with your physical senses tunes you up for seeing and sensing beyond the physical, so that you can be a more accurate instrument for your intuition to perceive the signs of the Universe.

Feel Your Feelings: Stop Suffering

Long time ago, an old *curandera* said to me: *"What you can name, you can heal."* In other words, when you recognize the energetic patterns of your disempowering feelings and their triggers, you can shift them. Then they don't linger and create a vibrational story that hooks the Universe into creation. When you dare to feel your feelings, especially uncomfortable feelings, you can move through them. Even better, when you recognize them, you can interrupt the pattern and refocus your energy. It is very natural to try to avoid feelings that cause pain, because . . . who wants to suffer? But as the saying goes, what you resist persists. It is exactly the resistance that causes the suffering.

When we don't want to feel the pain, we push against the feeling. It gets stuck and take over our energy system. When we rationalize, explain and justify any heavy feeling that makes us suffer, we get more and more stuck in a limiting pattern or a story. Hoping the feeling lifts, while we push against it, is like closing our eyes and hoping for the best right before something hits us.

Eventually, the story of pain becomes a habitual field. We believe that story single-mindedly because it *feels* so real. We identify with it. We defend it. We are officially suffering.

Naming your pain and recognizing its triggers help you regulate your feelings so that you don't remain trapped in a web of a story that feeds itself through a fear-based thought-feeling-thought-loop. Observe your body and consciously straighten your back. Breathe deeply. Shift your posture to embody confidence. Distract yourself from the limiting story loop. Distracting means focusing your energy and thought in a new way that makes you feel lighter. An excellent way to explore this is the test of heavy or light. Ask yourself: "Does this thought make me feel lighter or heavier?" Or "What thought could I choose to think to feel lighter, instead?" Or "What energy do I need to be to shift this into a better feeling state?"

Resistance is a form of fear. Seeing this clearly and taking responsibility of your feelings and your own well-being help you pull yourself out of the story and out of suffering. You can train yourself to see it as a choice and as a decision. It is a choice between being a victim or a creator.

When you learn to choose to be free to love, accept, honor, and value yourself, it becomes natural to extend kindness, compassion, and love to those around you who are acting out because they are still suffering.

What Do You Need Right Now?

Those who have worked with me one on one or in groups know that my first question often is: *"What do you need?"* I ask it, so that you learn to ask it of yourself regularly. In taking care of yourself as a sensing, feeling, thinking, intuitive whole, this question is basic. When you are in touch with your own needs, you can fulfill them.

We are conditioned to look outside for our needs to be met, so that often we don't even know what our needs are. Instead, there might be a general sense of something missing—a sense of wanting, of yearning, of not knowing. As a child you have to rely on others, as an adult, it is essential you reclaim your power. When you learn to count on yourself for nurturing, support, and caring for your needs, you can be healed and empowered.

What if you could learn to be there for yourself? Then you wouldn't have to depend on anybody else's capacity to love or to understand. Truth to be told, nobody will ever really "understand" or "get" you. Their business is to be there for themselves. However, when you are in touch with your own needs, you show up in the world more balanced and whole. Understanding how seeking to fulfill your needs affect your behavior, you learn how you can clear any unbalanced behavior. As you honor your own needs, you learn to honor others' needs as well.

Sometimes you need to be assertive and decided, other times soft and gentle. Know when to demand more and when to relax and nurture. Sometimes you need to shout out loud, other times to allow the silence to speak.

What if you honored your needs and learned to love yourself so deeply that you could offer your 100 percent of wholeness and unconditional love to everyone in your life, regardless of their ability or inability to love, give, or receive? How would that be for you?

In everyone's childhood there are bound to be disappointments, limitations and misunderstandings, and sometimes also true violations of the child's safety and trust. There is a powerful video in which Oprah talks with Bishop TD Jakes about parents' capacity to love. He explains how we have these ideals of how a mother should be or how a father should be, and how we might be waiting for all our lives for them to "get" it and love us. Bishop Jakes says to Oprah (I paraphrase), *"What if you are born with a ten-gallon capacity to love and you show up in a family of pint-sized people? Even if they give you their everything, they will never know how to fill you up, because you are bigger than that."*

This is not to say the "pint-sized people" are inferior. Perhaps the people in your family gave up on themselves. Perhaps they too began with ten-gallon capacity to love, but as children they were victimized in some way and their capacity slowly was reduced or even entirely depleted. What if we chose those parents exactly for the opportunity to learn to love ourselves? When you love yourself deeply and unconditionally, you can afford to forgive deeply and to love unconditionally and discern who are the ones that matter in your life. Receive love from where it is, rather than insist on looking for it where it is not.

What is the essence of what you need? Look behind and beyond whatever you feel or think you need. There are the basic human needs, such as air, water, food, shelter, sleep. But then there are other physical, psychological, emotional and spiritual needs, such as love, belonging, security, certainty, significance, self-actualization, feeling of service, creativity, contribution to a greater good, personal and spiritual growth.

Let's look at a simple example. What if you say you need a vacation? Is that a need? Whatever you say you need, look behind it. What does needing a vacation reveal to you? How could you fulfill the energetic need of a vacation without actually taking a vacation? What does vacation mean to you? Perhaps you could take more conscious moments throughout the day to daydream, to raise your vibration, to go for a long walk, to be a tourist in your own town, to watch a movie, to read a book, to make a delicious new dish for dinner. Use your imagination to give yourself an experience with the essence of vacation. Be open to receiving it and being nurtured wherever you are.

If you are an extrovert or an introvert, your needs of a

vacation are surely very different. Having very different needs can lead to misunderstanding, confusion, conflict, and judgment. Being an introvert, I once had a boyfriend, who was an extrovert. To charge his batteries, he wanted to party and be in a huge group of people with loud music. To charge mine, I wanted to have a quiet dinner and deep conversation in candlelight just with him. And mind you, he was totally shy if put in a spotlight in front of an audience, whereas I would easily take the spotlight and lead thousands of people on a journey with me on big stages.

When you first meet someone, you wear pink glasses and are happy to do anything with them and for them, but only when you know yourself and your own needs in a conscious way, can you honor both yourself and others. You free yourself by releasing any rigid patterns that limit you and put conditions to your happiness. Allow your needs to be taken care of in creative ways.

What if you could be fulfilled in surprising new ways that make you equally happy and equally honor your deepest needs?

There is a story of a princess who wanted to marry a prince. She wanted him to be an amazing human being with a long list of carefully specified "must-have" qualities. Furthermore, the princess wanted him to arrive on a white horse. One beautiful day, this most amazing prince, a beautiful human being, arrived at the castle to ask for the hand of the princess in marriage. He fulfilled her list to a tee, with some other extraordinary, unique qualities that she had not imagined even in her wildest dreams. He was willing to love and honor the princess and live happily ever after with her . . . however, he arrived on a black horse.

What do you think our princess did? She rejected him.

The truth is, when you learn to recognize your true needs, you will also recognize your dream, even if it arrives on a black horse.

PLAY WITH THE UNIVERSE

As you play with the Universe, remind yourself to use all your senses to create rituals throughout the day. Here you find a simple, powerful visualization to elevate your vibration, expand your vision and to communicate with the Universe. You can use this same kind of visualization to support others.

In the journaling you may explore your dominant feelings and your needs more intimately for your ultimate wholeness, integrity and freedom.

Visualization of the Highest Light

When you hold yourself or anyone else in the highest light and unconditional love, you always hold space for the highest and best outcome. This shifts your vibrational space instantly. The more vividly you imagine with all your senses, the faster and more profound the shift is.

See Yourself in Your Highest Light

This is a powerful way to program your body and brain to a new state of being and to honor your commitment to your new vision and story.

Take a moment every day to imagine yourself as luminous, happy and smiling, in radiant health and in perfect flow with the Universe. Imagine with all your senses the highest possible vision for yourself at this time. Direct your mind, energy and attention into seeing yourself with the eyes of the Universe. You are held, honored and expanded by the highest light of consciousness. Magnify your vision with more light. Breathe. Smile. See yourself as joyous, confident, fulfilled, free, and at peace. Praise yourself. Tell yourself what you need to hear to be supported, nurtured or inspired: *"You are amazing. I am proud of you. You can do anything. I see you in your highest light."*

Listen to the Universe echoing back to you: *"You are infinitely supported."*

Hold Space and See Others in Their Highest Light

I am often asked how to help a loved one who is in any kind of trouble, especially if you feel helpless or worried and don't know what to do. First, make sure you don't think about them with worry and concern, but instead consciously begin seeing anyone you love or wish to support in their highest light.

See them through the eyes of love.

Hold space for them and see them as filled with light, happy and at peace. Trust that they are held and guided by the highest light and infinite wisdom. This vision creates an energy and vibration of support, healing and empowerment.

Instead of trying to help or fix, holding space this way means accompanying the person in their journey with nonjudgmental support. This is a gentle space to allow them to simply be, and to feel safe, loved, accepted, and not alone. It is a state of listening, where you don't want or need anything back. It is honoring the person's truth and path with a compassionate heart and gentle presence without an opinion. Imagine offering a space of acceptance, with no judgment or conditions. Imagine the person being received, heard, seen, and loved without having to deserve it in any way.

Holding space says: *"I am here for you. Take your time."* Love and acceptance say: *"I see you in your highest light."*

Journal to Shift Your Story

Allow the journaling ideas to inspire you as a starting point, but feel free to follow the lead of your own intuition. Pay attention to what your own guidance invites you to explore as you look into our feelings, needs and values.

Name Your Feelings

Name your most dominant feelings. Come up with at least five empowering, energizing or inspiring feelings and also five disempowering, discouraging or disheartening feelings that you recognize as part of your day to day repertory. You are welcome to come up with more emotions and feelings, but it is most useful when they are feelings you encounter in your everyday life. Imagine you are a method actor or actress, explore each feeling from both groups:

- How does it feel in your body? Where do you feel it? When you feel this, how do you carry yourself? What does your face look like?
- Act it out. How does it affect your breath? Your voice?
- What is the story that triggers it?
- Does it feel heavy or light? Energy up or down? Does it move you forward or hold you back?
- Which feelings have the most power to affect your state of being?
- Do you define yourself through any of these feelings? *I am like this.*

Journal about your reflections. The purpose of this exploration of feelings is to help you recognize what your feelings are and how they are triggered, so that you can learn to focus your energy and consciously choose empowering feelings rather than disempowering ones.

What Do You Need?

Knowing what you need is an important and powerful part of your self-discovery.

- Can you name your top three physical, psychological and emotional needs? What is the order of priority?
- Are there needs you are expecting to be fulfilled by someone else?
- Think of any of your needs. How can you give the essence of that need to yourself today?

What Is Most Important for You in Life?

What do you value most in life? Why?

Based on your values, what is a deal-breaker in friendship or in a romantic relationship?

To explore your values helps you understand your dominant story and your choices. It is also helpful to remember that everyone makes their choices according to *their* values, which might be very different from yours.

Your Wisdom Book

Making these wisdom notes helps you perceive the world through new eyes and create a new conditioning for your life. You already know, when you actively look for inspiration, you train your brain to look for more of it in your life.

- Find an inspiring quote or a poem that fits the themes we are exploring and write it in your wisdom book.
- Write at least three things you are grateful for. Make appreciation a habit. As you write them, say them out loud with deep feeling.

- What message stands out specifically for you at this time from reading this chapter? This should be something that hooked your attention and felt important. Formulate your insights in your own words. Allow it to be a message from your inner guidance.

Instant Shift Tip: Snap Out of It

This little technique is best done standing. It is perfect for those moments when you need some help regrouping immediately.

Snap your fingers and take a step out of the space where you were standing. If you cannot snap your fingers, clap your hands.

After you have taken the step out of the space, you may also clear the space with three upward swipes with your hands. Imagine sweeping the energy up into the recycling center on the Universe. Use your breath to direct the energy.

FOUR

TRUST YOUR INTUITION, TRUST YOUR SIGNS

What you don't know, you don't need to know.

W ould you be willing to let go of your need to control?

It is mostly your need to control that gets in the way of trusting your guidance. The need to control feels pretty much like being out of control, doesn't it?

Your inner and outer reality reflect active programs running in your energy system. To gain clarity, we often ask for signs to guide us and to direct us to "right" choices, but instead of gaining the clarity we want, we end up more confused—because we ask conditionally. We are pushing for an answer, fighting reality, wanting to control or fix the story. When we want a sign or an answer desperately, it usually blocks any useful information from coming to us. When we are energetically broadcasting fear, doubt, or insecurity in any form, there cannot be a transmission of peace, clarity, or insight at the same time. This is why it is so important to tend to our vibration first.

As you enter the space of stillness within, your figuring-out mind will quiet down, you can begin to see clearer and to trust your knowing.

Teach yourself to pay attention to insights, ideas, perceptions, observations, dreams, feelings, thoughts, sensations, and anything else that hooks your attention. All of the above could bring you information and are part of your navigation system. The more you train yourself to use your awareness, the clearer you will see, hear, or otherwise perceive the answers you are seeking. The answers are always there, but you might not be in a vibrational space to receive or see them yet.

While it is fine to study the meanings of the signs and symbols or look them up in books or on the internet, always discern and trust yourself. You will notice there are often many explanations and interpretations. Your signs are those which resonate with you and have personal meaning for you. Trust your own knowing. You are the expert in *your* sign language, and always the ultimate interpreter of your signs.

I have a friend with an intricate system of decoding accurate information relating to the chakra system from license plates. Her system would not make sense to anyone else. Another friend has her toes twitch and tingle as a confirmation of any question.

Someone I know had to make a six-figure proposal for an amazing opportunity to offer his expertise to the world. He had no idea what figure to ask, so he went for a walk on the beach and asked to be given a certain kind of rare feather for each hundred thousand dollars he was supposed to ask. He picked quite a few of them that morning and asked for the exact amount the feathers indicated. To his surprise, it was precisely the figure they were willing to pay.

Five people can see the same white feather and receive a different personal message from it. One might know that angels are near, another interprets it as a sign of peace, a third one sees it as hope, fourth one is ready to take flight and finds the feather as a symbol of freedom, and the fifth one knows that his or her payers has been answered. Oh, and we already know the sixth one who got hundreds of thousands of dollars according to his feathers. We can go on with a list of meanings, also you might be all of these people at different moments. Allow any sign to reveal its unique message every time in each moment.

Trusting your intuition goes hand in hand with trusting, knowing and valuing yourself. The more you understand how your personal energy-consciousness system works, the better able you will be to distinguish the voice of your intuition from the voice of doubt or a limiting story.

With practice and simple noticing, you'll learn to trust yourself and your signs, and to discern what belongs to you and what belongs to others. You will see what is or isn't your responsibility. You learn trust yourself in taking action without a limiting attachment to the outcome.

I grew up with the Serenity Prayer. Perhaps its simple truth will help you as well.

God grant me the serenity to accept the things I cannot change, courage to change the things I can, and the wisdom to know the difference.

One day, after taking a yoga class in Miraflores, Lima, I was walking home feeling very grounded, and yet flowing with the Universe. I stopped walking for a moment and closed my eyes because a line from a song popped into my head: *"Hello, is it me you're looking for?"* My consciousness expanded and I saw myself soaring among the stars, literally playing with the Universe. It felt wonderful.

Still aware that I was on a street in a big city, I opened my eyes, thinking I would continue my astral journey later, back at home. Right at that moment a taxi came down the street. The driver looked at me with a big smile on his face. On the side of his car there were big letters reading: TAXI ASTRAL. I had to laugh out loud.

Another similar story comes to mind. Once, I was walking through the West Village in New York City, making plans for my life. I looked up at the sky and asked the angels to show me that they were there with me. I hoped to receive assistance in cleansing my energy field of any residue from the past.

A second later, my path was blocked by a huge white van. On the side it read: ANGELO'S CLEANING SERVICE.

Keep your eyes open and listen, the Universe is talking to you, and often with a sense of humor and playful lightness.

Your Body as a Truth-o-Meter

Your body can serve as a Truth-o-Meter to help you trust the information you get. Listen to your body. Learn to know its subtle ways of communication. It is an amazing miracle composed of trillions of cells. There are more cells in your body than there are stars in our Milky Way galaxy. In our extraordinary physical system, each cell receives information accurately through various chemical signals and responds to messages from its surroundings. Your brain and heart in sync with every other organ and each system in your body work extraordinarily together constantly communicating with the field of consciousness of the Universe.

By paying attention to how you feel physically, you can learn to read subtle changes and recognize and trust the significance of certain sensations in your body. The clearer you are, the better you begin to distinguish your body's way of talking to you. As always, every tool you use gets better with practice.

A subtle change in any part of your body may indicate that your Truth-o-Meter is signaling you. Personally, I get shivers all over when I need to pay attention to what is happening, and they intensify when there is a definite shift to lighter energy with more freedom, or when the matrix of possibility changes. If I am talking to a client and get shivers and goosebumps, for instance, I will let the client know that something is happening. When I do, more often than not, the client also feels a clear sensation. When the matrix of possibility changes, it means there are more choices. The playfield opens up. When we are vibrating low, there don't seem to be many, if any, choices.

Not everything is figure-out-able, so honor your truth, flow in the now, and learn to trust your knowing. Allow your intuition to bring you information in surprising ways. Be light and lightness. Keep playing.

Find out if your physical body is a reliable tool of sensing for you. If it is, your ultimate aim should be to trust and have full confidence in your physical feedback. When asked, *"When do you know you can trust yourself with signs and sensations?"* I always answer, *"When you don't need to ask."*

Remember, there is no absolute truth, only your interpretation of what is.

Play with asking simple yes or no questions. Try different ways, such as imagining a billboard on a stadium with either yes or no lighting up, perhaps blinking. It could even be with sound and cheers from the audience for yes, and boos for no.

Or imagine a traffic light, showing green for yes, red for no, and yellow for neutral, which might happen if perhaps it was not the right time for an answer.

Ask your body: *"Show me yes."* And see if you have a sensation. When you ask it to show you no, notice if it is distinguishable enough from yes for you to rely on. When asking your first yes or no questions, begin with something obvious, so that you have little or nothing at stake. Ask for example: "*Am I a woman, yes or no?*" Or "*Am I a man, yes or no?*" Imagine a billboard, traffic light, or any other way you are playing with, showing you the answer.

Personally, I would certainly hope that the answer is "yes" to being a woman in my case, otherwise I know I cannot trust myself with this tool at the moment. It is an indication for me to tend to my vibration and to center and focus my being into the present moment.

You already know that before you ask for a sign or any question, it is always best to take a moment to clear your thoughts, ground yourself, and become a space of possibility.

Before you ask what that means, allow your imagination to show you. Ask it: "*How would it feel to be a space of possibility?*"

Other Tools of Knowing

There are many divination tools that you might feel called to explore. Check in with yourself and feel which one resonates with you. One that I like is a simple pendulum. To me, it is a fast way to check if a choice coincides with my gut feeling. At the time of writing this book, I was attracted to working with clear quartz, so I used a clear quartz pendulum.

Trust your intuition as to what kind of pendulum you would like. And remember that you don't need a special one; you can literally use anything that hangs and has a little weight to it, including a necklace or your keys on a reasonably long chain. Perhaps you would like to make one for yourself.

If you are new to pendulum, begin by holding the pendulum still and saying: "*Show me yes.*" Then "*Show me no.*" Both times wait for it to move. Your pendulum might move sideways or swing forward and back. It might spin in a clockwise or counterclockwise circle. There is no rule. The requirement of course is for the two signs to be different.

For me, the movements have remained the same for yes and no since I first asked; it has made no difference if I was using a formal pendulum or a homemade device.

I have an additional little ritual I do every time before asking a yes or no question on my pendulum. I invite my highest guides to be present, and as a confirmation they are with me, the pendulum makes a circle. This sign came about when I asked for the first time if my guides were present. The pendulum went in circles, instead of my usual diagonal yes. Actually, it has never happened that they would not be there. In fact, they are always with you.

Should a pendulum not move for you, try another one. If it doesn't move either, it might be an indicator that it is not your tool at this time.

I once had a pendulum made of Machu Picchu serpentine stone for sale with many other similar ones at a body-mind-spirit festival. At some point it was brought to my attention that this particular one was not moving for anyone. Many people had tried it, but it just stood still. How curious, I thought to myself, but the moment I hung it, this pendulum started swinging so fast it almost flew out of my fingers. Needless to say, this serpentine pendulum is very dear to me. When choosing a pendulum, you might ask: *"Are you my pendulum? Yes or no."* In the case of the serpentine pendulum, it chose me.

As we talked before, test first with simple, easy, no-brainer questions. Once you trust you are getting consistent, reliable answers, you may choose to ask other more meaningful yes or no questions. Again, even then begin with lightness and playfulness, not going directly to the most earth-shattering and life-changing questions.

In fact, when everything is at stake, or when I am in desperate need for answers for myself, I never go to a tool such as the pendulum, or any other divination. When we are not centered, we cannot trust the answers. We are too invested emotionally, thus vibrationally off. On such occasions, my pendulum or billboard would happily confirm that indeed, I am a giraffe.

Expand Your Awareness

Once in Cusco, Peru, I started talking with a man claiming to be a shaman. He immediately made it clear that he was a "shaman," something that an actual Peruvian shaman would not do. I was curious because I spotted his inauthenticity right away, yet his voice was beautiful. His eyes were warm and beautiful. He had long, shiny, raven-black hair. He was wearing a colorful poncho. His features were noble, his presence calm and soothing, his manner kind and caring. He was charming and handsome. But I knew he was lying.

The man started "reading" my energy, no permission asked. I let him, because by this time he had become the subject of my investigation. He told me all kinds of stuff about the colors in my aura. The main point being that, according to him, I was in desperate need of cleansing and protection which he, of course, could provide me for a fee. He told me he would make an amulet, a talisman of protection, for me and he would receive me at his house up in the mountain for cleansing.

Why I wanted to share this story with you is that, in his case, even though I knew with 100 percent certainty that this man was an insincere, deceitful con artist, there was a part of me that wanted to believe him. Even though I fully and completely trusted my own intimate knowledge about the state of my energy and aura, a part of me wanted to believe this charlatan. His tremendous talent was the art of seduction.

He wasn't sleazy. He never went over the line of being pushy. His language was cultivated, not crude. He was energetically trapping me. Only I wasn't trappable.

We left the matter at *"I'll think about it."* I had played my part of a blond tourist to perfection. By then, I had already lived in Cusco for a few years. When I got home, I thought about what it would have been like if I had been a traveler seeking answers, looking for my spiritual path, vulnerable, and with a wide-open heart, like so many who come to

Cusco. Would I have fallen under the spell of his very expert deception?

The man targeted mystical seekers with a skillful web of "trustworthiness," portraying himself as a protector and a healer. He used to have a shop in the Plaza of San Blas, but it's not there anymore. Because of the shop I was able to check him out on the internet that same day, and sure enough there were dozens of negative comments and warnings about him from women from all over the world, amongst them some who had fallen prey to his seduction, buying both the amulet and a "cleansing."

What surprised me in reading these reports was that his imagination was rather poor: He had described the colors in everyone's aura, including mine, in exactly the same way.

Not just with handsome "shamans," but with everyone in every situation, expand your awareness, trust your knowing. It is better to be too careful than the contrary. If you have one iota of doubt, pay attention. The better you know yourself, the clearer your intuition will become, and the better you will be able to read its nudges.

Your Truth-o-Meter is great not only for sussing out a deception, but also for discerning everything fabulous that is flooding into your awareness and experience.

Do You Recognize a Sign when You See It?

You might have heard the story of the man who had blind faith in God. One day, an urgent warning was issued to evacuate his home because of a fast-rising, torrential flood that had already destroyed half the town.

This man decided to stay. He said to himself, *"I put my trust in God. I know he will save me."*

The neighbors were leaving, and they offered him a ride in their car. But the man responded, *"No thank you, God will save me."*

The water was indeed rising fast and the man had to go to the second floor of his house. Someone came to the window in a boat and said: *"Come quickly! There is room for the two of us in my boat."* But our man responded, *"No thank you, God will save me."*

Now the man had to climb up onto his roof. It was slippery. The water was rising even faster. A rescue helicopter carrying emergency personnel was circling above the flooded town when they spotted this man balancing on a rooftop. They dropped a ladder with a rescue worker reaching out his hand. *"C'mon, I've got you. Take my hand. I won't let go of you. You are safe."* But once again, the man looked up to the sky and said: *"Thank you, but no. God will save me."*

The rescue worker witnessed the man being swept away by the raging waters. With his last, dying breath, the man shouted: *"Why didn't you save me, God? I believed in you. I had faith in you all my life. I put all my trust in you."*

An answer came from the heavens. *"I tried. I sent you a warning, a car, a boat, and a helicopter, but every time you refused my help."*

Signs can give us an unexpected answer. Often, we insist

on our preconceived ideas of not only signs, but everything else in life as well. We create limiting expectations, and like the man in the story, or the princess, whose prince arrived on a black horse – we reject it.

In other words, we fail to see the door opening, while staring at a closed door. It is very human to keep fighting against something, while its opposite is also available. We are conditioned that way. Only you can break that conditioning for yourself.

We look for signs when we want answers or clarity. We hope a sign will relieve us of our confusion. A paradox is that when we are most desperate for guidance, we are usually in a place vibrationally where we cannot perceive signs or guidance. We would be unable to see a sign, even if it were right in front of us.

I know, I have been there. I've missed plenty of signs.

We often miss even the most obvious signs because we want a certain sign, or we don't really want to see signs in the first place, only get confirmations for what we already believe. We often feel the need for approval and validation, so we listen to people around us, rather than tap into our own innate genius, wisdom, and knowing for answers.

Trust Yourself

A few years ago, I was back in New York right after I had been to Peru for the first time and I felt like something bigger was cooking for me there. My soul was calling me. I had gone to Peru following strong signs, fulfilling a promise I had made to myself at age thirteen. My whole trip felt as if it had been orchestrated from above. When the wheels of the plane touched down on Peruvian soil, I felt deeply stirred and burst into tears. All sorts of doors started opening for me in Peru. My connection to the Andes Mountains felt ancient, yet alive and vibrant. I had peace in my heart like never before, and at the same time strangely unsettled.

Right away, I felt so at home in Cusco, with a familiarity that is impossible to explain. Even my body felt at ease at the altitude of 11,200 feet (3,400 meters). Mind you, I grew up at sea level in Finland, a very flat country where a hill of a few hundred feet or meters is considered to be a mountain.

You would think that at this point there was no need to question my relationship with Peru. The signs could not have been clearer. But no, I still needed some reassurance. So, I set up an appointment with a lady who does angel readings. She came highly recommended by a trusted friend.

The angel lady began her reading with very general information. I was impatiently waiting for my answers—I was impatient because I already knew the answers. The more she talked, the less her words resonated with me. She started to speak some financial jargon about diversified portfolios. At this point, I was listening with increasing irritation. I even said: *"Where are you getting this stuff? This cannot be from my angels. They know my language and how to talk to me. I don't understand a word you are saying."* Nor was I too interested to listen beyond that point.

She insisted that all the information was from my angels. I thought there must have been a change of staff in the invisible realm because I barely knew anything about portfolios. I didn't have any assets to diversify. I asked her to please change the topic.

She said, *"You travel a lot."* Okay, now we were talking. I was still vibrating from the soul expansion of Peru. Testing her, I asked if she saw any specific countries in my future. She said: *"Absolutely. Sweden and Belgium come through very strongly."* My jaw dropped. Sorry Sweden and Belgium, but at that moment, if I'd had to list all the countries in the world I probably would not have even remembered that these existed.

I then asked her directly about Peru. Almost angrily she said that Peru was not for me—absolutely not. At that point, I ended the call as politely as I could muster.

I was ranting to myself: *"What a waste of money. She doesn't know anything. She's not in touch with anything. How can she claim to read my angels or any angels? What was my friend thinking? Why would anyone recommend her?"* And then, all of a sudden, I tangibly felt like someone was tickling me. There was this light, playful, giggling energy in the room. It was like my angels were laughing and high-fiving each other over the practical joke they had pulled on me.

They *had* been feeding information to this well-meaning lady. *Wrong* information. I had to laugh out loud.

Today, I consider this woman a major sign and a messenger for me. She gave me a powerful message, just not what I expected, but it was exactly the message I needed.

The message from my guides was clear: "*You already have the answers you seek.*"

You can ask directly from your angels, or the Universe, or however you choose to play it. You may also ask a wise friend, a healer, an angel reader, a therapist, or a coach to hold space for you. Sometimes you may need more help with asking the best questions, so that it is easier for you to see, recognize, and acknowledge your true answers.

I absolutely recommend having a coach or a guide for direction and as a sounding board, but ultimately trust yourself. Others cannot give you absolute answers or tell you what to do. Only you can.

A Good Sign or a Bad Sign?

Collectively, we are conditioned to prepare for the worst and taught to look for signs of bad things coming. For what? To avoid a disaster. You might think you are protecting yourself by anticipating the other shoe dropping, but you could end up "protecting" yourself from prosperity and happiness too in the process.

What if you committed to preparing for best-case scenarios, and began looking for signs to support those instead?

Signs themselves are neither good nor bad, it is the

meaning you give them and your interpretation that make them so.

What if you began to tell a new story all together, where you let go of the whole good-bad polarity?

There is an old story about a farmer, a widower, who lived in a humble home with his only son and an old horse to work his fields. One day his horse ran away, and his neighbors said: "*Oh, how terrible. Such bad luck that your horse escaped.*"

The old man responded: "*Good luck, bad luck, who knows?*"

A week later, the old horse returned with a herd of wild horses following it. This time the neighbors who came by were a little envious. They congratulated the farmer on his amazingly good luck. Again, he responded: "*Good luck, bad luck, who knows?*"

Then, when his son was mounting one of the untamed horses, the boy fell badly and broke his leg. The neighbors came with their condolences, again lamenting how terribly bad luck to have his only son break his leg. But the farmer only said: "*Good luck, bad luck, who knows?*"

A little later, the army marched into the village, drafting all the young men to go to war. The farmer's boy was spared because of his broken leg. Good luck? Bad luck?

What is the moral of the story for you? To me, it is about allowing space to see things from a wider perspective before rushing into a definite final conclusion. It is good to stay centered with what is without projection or judgment. We often don't know why things have to happen. We only see the big picture later, and perhaps can understand things only in retrospect. The old farmer didn't ever go into a story about what was happening. He stayed present, minding his business, pivoting as needed with what life gave him at any given moment.

I Choose to See Good Signs

Once in Cusco, I was walking near the inca ceremony site Saqsaywaman with Benito, a pampamisayoq who is a friend of mine. A *pampamisayoq* is an Andean shaman. We were on our way to do a ceremonial offering for Pachamama. *Pachamama* is the Andean name for Mother Earth. I love how *pacha* in the local language, Quechua or *runasimi,* means not only "earth," but also "universe," "cosmos," "time," and "space." So Pachamama can also be understood as the Mother of the Universe, or Cosmic Mother.

Walking with Benito on this winding path above the City of Cusco made me feel aware, alive, and present, as if we had all the time and space in the world.

I pointed out to Benito, *"Look! What a beautiful bird!"*

He smiled and said: *"A good sign."*

"Look what I found," I said, holding a crystallized rock in my hand.

He said: *"A good sign."*

A flower. *"A good sign."*

A bird song. *"A good sign."*

After many, many, many good signs, I asked him, *"Benito,*

are there any bad signs?"

He just smiled. No answer.

That was my sign. It became totally clear to me that I can at any given time choose to see a sign and also choose it to be a good sign. We do have that freedom, first, to choose to pay attention and to see the signs, and second, to interpret and decode the signs through our own intuition and ways of knowing. That day, walking on a winding path behind Saqsaywaman in my beloved mountains in Cusco, was the day I decided to choose to see *only* good signs.

When I talk about "good" signs, I don't necessarily mean "good" versus "bad" in the most obvious sense. I am not talking about judgment in a moral sense of good versus evil. I am simply inviting you to choose the best interpretation of any sign, an interpretation that serves and supports you, and enables your understanding to expand sufficiently so that you can see how, in the big picture, a hardship can also be a blessing. Not only responding with the laconicism of the farmer (*Good luck, bad luck, who knows...*), but by actively trusting and consciously deciding to find the embedded gift. This is a choice that empowers you. It is a choice that can give you peace.

I Followed a Sign, but It Didn't Work Out

There might be times when you question a sign because you are not getting what you expected. You received the sign for Mr. or Ms. Right *Now*, for example, but you interpreted the sign in every possible way so as to convince yourself that it was for Mr. or Ms. Right. You wanted to believe it so much that you married the person, perhaps even wishing secretly that she or he would change, and then it wasn't happily ever after.

The reason why manifestation sometimes works out easily is that we are not attached to the outcome. Our happiness doesn't depend on the outcome. We will be at peace no matter what. When things don't work out, we are usually not a vibrational match with what we wish to manifest. There are beliefs, patterns, and habits that push our manifestation in the opposite direction of our desired outcome.

Consciousness responds to our vibration. If we are attached to the outcome, we try to force it rather than being open to it. In creation, there is no trying. "Trying" pushes everything away. As does "wanting." It is always somewhere out there. Instead of trying and wanting, choose.

You are not here just for that one job, or to get married or to prove your worthiness to anyone. You are here to learn to love, so that you can answer your soul's call and choose from the infinite possibilities of your soul path. As you raise your vibrational frequency, your matrix of possibility shifts. You have more choices and your ability to see the bigger picture is heightened.

Imagine you are looking down at your entire life, as if from a mountaintop, and you have a magical telescope that makes it possible for you to zoom into every moment of your life.

You see every choice and sign from a higher perspective. Here and now is your point of power.

What if the signs you received in the past brought you right here?

What if every event in your life held a gift and a meaning for this moment?

What if you were exactly where you were meant to be now and always?

PLAY WITH THE UNIVERSE

As you play with the Universe and journal about it, you begin to see guidance and signs everywhere. The more you quiet your mind and tend to your state of being, you can be guided in the now, not only in retrospect.

Journal to Shift Your Story

By exploring your own stories, you learn to see the big picture and to trust your intuition to guide your way.

Easy Manifesting

Think of a moment when manifesting something was easy for you, a time when you both asked and received. How was it different from other times? Journal about the experience. Examine the details and how this same formula could be replicated.

Your Gut Feeling

Think of a few incidents in which your gut feeling was right. How did it feel? How did you "know" what you knew?

Did you have a sensation, hear words, see an image?

How would it have turned out had you not followed your gut feeling?

How about any experiences when you went against your gut feeling? Write about those as well. What sign did you ignore or disbelieve?

The Gift of a Challenge

Think back to a challenging situation or a painful event that eventually led you to something much better or gave you an insight that changed your life. Go deep and allow your wisdom to show you new insights. Imagine telling that story to someone or even to an audience. Write out the whole story with as many details as you can.

Instant Shift Tips

Whenever you feel lousy, or low in energy, it is always a good idea to pause and breathe, and when you combine breath and sound together with intention, they create a powerful instant medicine.

Oxygen is the most important life sustaining element on our planet. Your breath oxygenates your cells, fills you with life force energy and anchors you into the flow of life in the present moment.

When in Doubt, Breathe

Breathe in through your nose as if you were smelling the fragrance of beautiful flowers. Then hold your breath for a few of seconds.

As you hold your breath, stay focused, yet relaxed and soft. Become the space between your inbreath and outbreath.

Breathe out through your mouth with a sound of relief *"Ahhh."* Smile.

That still point between inbreath and outbreath is your entrance point to the Universe. You access it by becoming conscious of it. Therein lies a tremendous creative power.

Instant Peace

Put your hands on your heart. Hum gently with your lips closed. Feel the resonance in your chest as if your hands were singing. Do this any time you want to quiet your mind, be at peace and bring yourself fully into the present moment.

When you are feeling your voice, it is impossible at the same time to be thinking and figuring out. You drop out of the story and into harmony and balance.

You may also direct the sound and resonance to any part of your body where there is tension or pain. If you ever have a headache, imagine directing the sound of your own voice to dissolve the pain and create a space of relief.

Remember, where attention goes, energy flows.

Your Wisdom Book

Keep your eyes open for wisdom every day. When you have an insight, write it in your wisdom book. If you haven't already, draw into it as well, if it inspires you.

- Draw a power sign for yourself in your wisdom book. You can practice it in your other journal. It can be as simple as a spiral, a star, a circle, anything.
- Write at least three gratitude statements. Anchor the feeling of appreciation and the vibration of thankfulness to your body as you write.
- What is the most important idea you want to remember from this chapter? Write it down, in your own words.

FIVE

THE UNIVERSE ALWAYS SAYS YES

What if everything was just a frequency away?

T o shift and to manifest, it is important to understand that we live in a vibrational universe. It is your vibration that hooks you up with consciousness and the creative power of the Universe. Whether you feel high or low, consciousness moves through you accordingly. The signs you see and your interpretation of them are part of the vibrational dance of the creation. The Universe is talking to you and you talk back to it, teaching it how to communicate with you and how to create with you.

The Universe is neutral. It is pure consciousness, which means it doesn't judge or evaluate. It doesn't blame or punish. The Universe is neutral the same way love is neutral. Not the conditional love of human drama, but the pure, unconditional, divine love. It just loves everything. It supports everything. In other words, the Universe always says yes. Love always says yes. Your responsibility is to choose what the Universe says yes to. Responsibility is your ability to respond. How are you responding to the infinite potentiality of the loving Universe? Are you free to rejoice in it? Do you love what you are creating?

Sometimes people ask if it is their fault that something is happening in their lives, or that something is not working out. I choose to think it being empowering to know that we can learn to focus our energy in a way that shifts our reality. It is exactly the limiting stories of blame, shame, guilt, and such that we want to shift. When we look at our story with clarity, compassion, and love, then we can consciously choose to commit to another story. Through our commitment, we pay attention to where we invest our energy. We can learn to focus our attention intentionally, consciously, so that we will not go back to the old story.

There is a story of an old man fishing on a bridge leading to a small village, where a big market was to be held for the following few days. Sellers from near and far came in the hope of good sales and trade. A man with a full-to-the-brim horse carriage stopped to talk with the old man. He asked: *"How is the village? How are its people? Are they friendly? Do they pay good prices? This is my first time here."*

The old man asked in return: *"How are people in your village?"*

"Oh, they are horrible. So stingy. They cheat," the man replied. *"You can't trust them. That is why I came here. I really hope it's different here."*

The old man smiled and answered: *"They are pretty much*

like that here too."

After a while, another man approached with a big horse carriage full of produce to sell. "Hello, old man, how are you today? How's the fish?"

"I'm good. All good."

"By the way, how are people in this town? I am new here. This is my first time."

"How are people in your village?" the old man asked.

"Oh, they are wonderful. We all work together. In fact, not all this produce is mine, I am hoping to sell some for my old neighbor too."

The old man smiled and said: "They are pretty much like that here too."

After the market ended, the old man was fishing again on the bridge. Out comes the first man with the full-to-the-brim horse carriage. He looked angry and shouted to the old man: "You were right. Just like in my village, the people were stingy, I hardly sold anything. See, my carriage is almost as full as before. A total waste of time. I will never come back."

Soon after came the second man, he stopped to greet the old man: "Hello friend, good to see you again. You were so right. The people in this village are wonderful. I sold everything, even for my neighbor. And I made lifelong friends and great trades. This was such a productive week. I will definitely come back. Thank you so much, my friend."

We see the world through the eyes of our dominant story, and always find proof for it everywhere we go.

Words Create

Most of the creation stories of the world tell of a word or a sound that held the power of creation. Words carry tremendous vibrational power. It pays to learn to command words with clarity.

Taste every word and feel its direction. As was discussed before, we often use the word *want,* but if you really feel into wanting something, how does it feel? You don't have it. You are actually resonating with lack. Be mindful of wanting.

The same with *hope.* While hope feels better than depression, it is not a good place to stay. Hope is a beggar. When you say, "I hope so," it almost feels there's very little hope. It keeps you waiting, wanting, hoping. I acknowledge hope is a needed steppingstone; however, allow it to lead the way to true empowerment and freedom. Pay attention to how you use words. The same word can be either empowering or disempowering, depending on the context and the energy you give it.

The more precise you are with your words, the clearer the focus of your creation.

When we say, *"I'm trying to be patient"* . . . translation: *"I could not be more impatient at the moment."* You either are or not, do or not, have or not.

If you are "trying" to shift, change, or transform your story, you go nowhere. There has to be a commitment, and when the shift actually happens, your life changes. Quietly.

Peacefully. Unannounced. You might notice later how you respond differently, how a trigger is no longer active. But the actual shift won't come with fireworks. "Trying" to transform is like "trying" to fall asleep (or in this case to awaken); when you wait for it, look for it, seek evidence of it, it cannot take place.

If you are "trying" to make more money, look carefully and with compassion, whether you might be coming to it from a feeling of lack, of not having enough. If you are "trying" to find the love of your life, look in the mirror and see if you can say: "*I love you*" to yourself and really mean it. If you are "trying" to get pregnant and have a hard time, see with the eyes of love if there is an underlying vibration of fear of not conceiving, or not carrying full term, or a lack of having a child.

If you have a "problem," how does it make you feel? Of course, it depends on the problem, but it probably feels anything from difficult and worrisome to hard and heavy. If you change the word *problem* to *challenge,* it most likely feels a little better. It might give you some energy to tackle a challenge. But what if, you chose to call it an opportunity? And ultimately—a gift.

To What Is the Universe Saying Yes?

Every thought and emotion create a vibrational contract with the Universe that sets a story and its creation in motion. Both the Universe and your neurological system will fire all the circuits to bring you whatever you vibrate.

Your vibration is determined by how you feel.

Whether consciously or by default, we are creating all the time. For some reason, we are often conditioned to oppose, to fight, to be against something that we don't want. Often it is much easier to know what we don't want. In that case, our focus and commitment are on what we don't want. We beat the drum of *"I don't want it. I don't want it. I don't want it."* We come up with justification and million reasons for why we need to fight it—and why everyone should fight it. We vibrate *not*-wanting with all our might.

There is tremendous energy invested in our opposition—energy we could use to heal, to transform, to create our dream lives. All the while, the neutral energy of the Universe, the field of potentiality, consciousness of all that is, was, and will be flows through us supporting us in not-wanting, reflecting back the proof and evidence of this-that-we-don't-want, using the RAS to filter only this-that-we-don't-want into our experience, thus keeping active this-that-we-don't-want in our system, so that we can continue not-wanting it.

Do you see how sneaky this is, how easily by accident we actually create more of what we don't want?

I love this message from Mother Teresa: *"I was once asked why I don't participate in anti-war demonstrations. I said that I will never do that, but as soon as you have a pro-peace rally, I'll be there."*

Let's be *pro* and *for*, rather than *anti* and *against*. I strongly feel that when we are for health and wholeness rather than against virus or cancer, or when we are for respect and understanding rather than against hatred and war—in fact, when we are *for* anything rather than against its opposite—we are more powerful as creators and human beings.

We can allow this-that-we-don't-want reveal to us what is on the other side of it. Not just to make a shift from not-wanting to wanting, which still keeps that-which-we-want out of reach, as we have discussed, but to shift directly to choosing, having, and being.

Everything Is Possible

What if I say to you that everything is possible? Do you say: *"Of course!"* and embrace this fact as energetic support for you on your path? Or is there a voice in your head that replies: *"What do you mean? I don't see it. It doesn't feel that way."* Perhaps someone has told you that this is not true, and you have accepted it as your truth.

Play with me. Say aloud to yourself, *"Everything is possible."* Taste it, feel it, imagine it.

Ask yourself: *"How would it feel if everything was possible?"* Did it change how you feel at all? You might think, *"It definitely is not possible for me to go to the moon (or to become a neurosurgeon, an opera singer, or grow wings and fly)."*

But I ask you: Is it your greatest calling to become an opera singer? Because if it is, you probably are studying music and giving it all you've got. Should you not succeed the way you expected or wanted, to pursue your soul's calling always serves a purpose.

The extreme and very public case of the New York heiress Florence Foster Jenkins and her deep desire to be a coloratura soprano is a good example. Did you see the brilliant and poignant movie about her that featured Meryl Streep and Hugh Grant?

Is it your heart's desire to go to the moon? If it is, I suspect you are in a space program somewhere, and if not an astronaut, cosmonaut, or intergalactic traveler, you might be an astrophysicist or astrophotographer.

Your calling calls you into you. The calling itself is a sign..

When you feel and imagine *"Everything is possible,"* what dreams are awakened in your heart? What is the direction your soul is pointing?

Feel the essence of your calling. What if there was not just one calling, but many? What if the essence of the calling was the key, the path? Find the deeper meaning of any journey. Find the gift. Your gift.

Within you is your very own "possible" that is being nurtured by your belief system and the story you tell. Check from time to time that your "possible" is not starving. Your possible is not absolute. It expands as you expand. It contracts as you contract.

Your dreams are signs. When you hear the whisper of a dream, a possibility that makes your heart sing, follow it, expand with it, trust it, and see where it leads you. When you commit to your true dream, nothing can stop you.

Many years ago, when still a doctoral student at The Juilliard School, I was in a rush-hour bus in Manhattan on a hot and humid, rainy day. Imagine the smell of wet and sweaty people in a packed bus. In came a lady who pushed herself into the crowded bus with a high-pitched, very entitled *"Excuuuse meee."* She elbowed me right in the ribs. It was not only annoying, but it hurt.

I took a big breath and was ready to swear in Finnish. Talking about using the power of sound and vibration, because unless there was a Finn in the bus, nobody would understand the exact word, yet the meaning behind the words would not be missed. At that moment, I was ready to give it to her with a powerful *RRR* sound. But then something came over me, a strange softness and gentleness. It was as if something stopped me from using this vibrational weapon. It was as if the irritation and frustration instantly melted away as well.

Right then, there was a tap on my shoulder. A kind looking lady behind me asked: *"Are you the flautist?"* I said that I am "a" flautist, yes. She said that she had attended one of my concerts and she then went on and on quoting me as saying something beautiful, powerful, wise, and profound during my performance.

The woman said: *"I have been going through a really rough time, but the resonance of your words and the sound of your flute have kept me going. Thank you so much. You gave me hope. You are an angel."*

Her outpour touched me deeply.

In fact, I think she is the angel of this story.

I got out of the bus and went to a park. I didn't care if it was raining. I looked up and said: *"Teach me, so that I can learn to walk my talk. So that I don't speak beautiful, powerful, wise words on stage and then lash out to someone who's having a bad day in a rush-hour bus. Teach me how to take full responsibility of my stuff."*

This encounter was one of the many signs on my path that eventually led me to study energy healing and all the wonderful tools that I am now sharing with you and the world through this book and other services I offer. It led me to learn to take responsibility for my end of the story, and not project my s@#$%t on anyone or anything.

It is common, when we are tired or low in energy, if someone, even a stranger, snaps at us, that we either snap right back at them or internally think, *"Why me? Why are they doing this to me?"* But when we are well-rested, well-nurtured, at peace, and full of energy, we might think: *"Poor thing, he's having a bad day. Blessings to you."*

Over time we can learn not to be triggered. Instead, we can choose to extend love and compassion to each other in any situation. That is when we know our story has shifted.

I am forever grateful for that rainy day when my path crossed for a second time with that lady. I was her sign at the concert. She was my sign on the bus. Both of our stories were shifted. What were the odds that we would be crammed together in a rush-hour bus in a city that's home to millions of people?

I am grateful for my healing practice, because it taught me early on that any kind of judgment had to stop. It would not be truthful to judge someone on the street and then be all light and love when they called me for a session. I had to take responsibility of my own actions, words, and energy. I also realized that the more conscious I become, the more powerful and focused the energy behind my words and actions was. This means that if I do swear, it now carries more poison than before. Every word, every action carries more power.

Of course, this doesn't mean that I don't ever get angry, frustrated, irritated, sad, or any other such thing, only that I know I don't have to hold on to those heavy feelings for a long time, or project them on others, or feel like a victim. I now know how to break the pattern and how to pull myself out of the limiting story.

How to Raise Your Vibration

It is as important to care for your vibration as it is to shower and to brush your teeth. You already know the Universe responds to your vibration, not merely to your words, prayers, requests or actions alone.

Life is good when we feel at ease and peaceful, when we see and feel with clarity and trust ourselves.

It is easy to overflow with gratitude, generosity, and heartfelt compassion towards the world when we are vibrating high. But what about when we are feeling low with irritation, worry, confusion, sadness, blame, or shame?

And what does it mean when we talk about a low versus a high vibration? Remember, the question: Does this make me feel heavy or light? You may ask: Does my energy go up or down? Heaviness indicates energy goes down. Everything feels hard, your vibration is dense, low, and slow. When you push against it, nothing seems to move, and nothing works no matter how much you try. It is exhausting. Even your body collapses. There is resistance all over it.

Obviously, you want to follow energy going up, filled with light, lightness and flow. Lightness feels like ease, grace, poise, and joy. You are inspired, energized, clear, and at peace. It is easy to trust and to surrender. It feels like everything always works out.

To raise your vibration, begin where you are. Allowing. Accepting. Breathing. Those are the keys. Pause for a moment and ask yourself: "*What do I need?*"

Sometimes you might need softening and relief. In those moments allow space for yourself to just be. Soften your heart to accept yourself as you are, nurturing especially the parts of you that feel the most rejected or undeserving of love and acceptance.

Other times you might need energizing and action through rigorous workout. Pump yourself up, shake your body, awaken every cell, find your strength. Shout out loud.

Begin seeing yourself confident, happy and smiling, radiant with your unique way of shining your light in the world. When you tune in and care for your vibration first, more of the universal matrix of potentiality becomes available to you, your own matrix of possibility expands.

Everything that makes you feel lighter, better, stronger, anything that makes you smile or fall in love with life, even a little bit, raises your vibration. Give space for acknowledging how far you have come. Celebrate your life and accomplishments. Use your imagination to fuel the story of your life with infinite possibility, playfulness, joy, inspiration, creativity, curiosity, sense of adventure, love, lightness, confidence, freedom, and gratitude.

When you shift your frequency and vibration, a new frequency becomes available for you. That is why I ask: *What if everything was just a frequency away?*

The Singing Flute

Some of you might know my story about asking for a sign in New York when I was close to finishing my studies at Juilliard. I remember it was a Sunday, a hot day in the middle of the summer, and I was thinking of my life and my dreams in my small shoebox apartment on the Upper West Side. That Sunday I was scared. I felt insecure about everything, feeling without direction, confused, no clarity. There was a dream brewing, I could feel it. I wasn't sure what it would look like, but I was assuming a performance career just like my peers and professors. Yet, something felt off.

Not long before, I had auditioned for a competition with high hopes only to be rejected because the total amount of votes was too low to advance to the live round. I got feedback from two anonymous judges, where one voted "yes," and said my recording was outstanding, absolutely winning material, original, and inspiring, and that I had made an interesting choice of repertory, showing courage and artistic independence. The other judge had written "no," with a short list of interpretation details he or she didn't agree on and made a comment about my use of vibrato in one spot. According to this person's taste, my choice of pieces was too weird.

As someone seeking validation and approval, guess which commentary I took more to my heart. Instead of hearing "outstanding and winning material," I heard "no and weird."

In those days I had been most on purpose, and felt most alive, when I did community outreach concerts, playing my flute in psychiatric wards, nursing homes, and the bedrooms of people in hospice care. There I felt humbled and empowered at the same time. I felt the authentic space of love, where the appreciation I received wasn't about my use of vibrato, but about the authenticity of my heart and my vulnerability. Those moments in which we sang and danced and prayed together as a human family were deeply moving, even life-changing. I will never forget how people in one of the mental wards I visited regularly started cheering as soon as I walked in: *"Yay, Ulla from Finland!"* Or when residents at a memory care senior home began singing a song we always sang together when they saw me.

They might not have remembered me, but they remembered the music and associated me with it. When memory fades, two things remain: love and music.

When I was playing at the bedside of the dying people, something just took over and played me. It wasn't about me. There was a blessing and sacredness and truth in those moments. Nothing to figure it out. Or to prove. Those countless moments of connection and love were what made me the musician that I am. That is the spirit I eventually learned to take with me on concert stages as well. So that even after a "regular" concert, someone might come to me and share how something shifted for them, or how their heart burst open.

On that particular hot summer Sunday on the Upper West Side in Manhattan, I felt lonely and miserable. I felt not good enough. On one level, I felt something greater calling, whispering, guiding me, whereas on another level, I didn't dare to trust it. When I thought about performing and being a musician, I assumed it would look like the career of my peers, colleagues, and professors. I felt I had a path, just couldn't figure out what it meant. I had witnessed the power of music and the blessing it can be, but if the career doors were closed, how would I be able to share that blessing with the world.

I didn't quite yet know who I was meant to be or what I was supposed to serve.

While I was performing and studying with the best people in the world, there was a missing piece.

I wasn't sure if I was on the right path.

We often think there is only right or wrong path, but there really is only a path. You are always exactly where you need to be. Your path is where you are. *Now* I know it.

Are you ever hesitant to make a choice because you are afraid to make a wrong choice?

We might freeze and end up not choosing anything at all. That's a passive choice, in fact. Perhaps you have felt confused, unclear, and insecure, just like I did on that particular Sunday.

That day, I decided to have a talk with the Universe. *"Hello,"* I said out loud by myself. *"I'm tired, I'm frustrated. I feel alone. I don't know what to do. And don't give me that 'listen-to-your-inner-wisdom' business because I don't hear a thing. And if I do, I cannot trust it. So, if I am to persevere, I am ready, but I need to know for sure that this is my path. And if this is not my path, let's change it right now. I don't care even if I finish my doctorate at Juilliard, I can do many things. So, here's the deal: Give me a sign! And give me a sign that I can understand. None of those cryptic messages that don't make any sense. Okay?"*

Silence.

On the one hand, I felt a bit better, I had vented to the Universe. On the other hand, I felt a bit shaken, because I had demanded a sign from the Universe. What if there was no sign after that? What if I missed it?

At this point, I was doubting everything. I went for a walk. I felt sad and lonely and lost and tired. As I was crossing Broadway at West 83rd Street, I saw a book on the ground in the middle of Broadway, upside down. One book. *"It must be someone's book,"* I thought, *"but, well, I can at least take a look."* I picked it up, turned it around, and saw the title of the book: The Singing Flute.

"Wow. Could this perhaps, maybe, be my sign?" I wondered. You see, it was not yet a strong enough sign for a flutist who had just demanded a sign from the Universe. However, fortunately, the story doesn't end there.

I had stated needing a clear sign that I could understand. I opened the book and read the first line: *"This is a story of a little Finnish girl . . ."*

I closed the book. Shaking at this point. *"Okay. You've got a deal. Show me the way."*

I have shared this story so many times because it illustrates how the Universe really is talking to us. In my case, at that time, I had been looking for other people's signs—the Juilliard students' signs, my professors' signs, my colleagues' signs—and totally missing my own, unique signs that were calling me to my own, unique purpose, which wasn't just to be a concert flutist, but to combine all my gifts and talents bestowed upon me into one path. Until I let go of my resistance and "trying" to figure it out, I wasn't able to see the guidance. It took that moment of desperation, where I didn't know any more what to do, for me to drop my resistance.

So, I surrendered. This is different from giving up. In surrendering you are only giving up your need to control, fix and figure things out.

Often surrender occurs in the moment when you have nothing to lose. When you are ready to say: I don't know what to do. *"Great,"* says the Universe, *"now there is space. Let's begin."*

Then you find the clarity to give up your limiting story, then you are ready to commit with all it takes to a new direction. Then you see how not advancing in a competition is perfectly in alignment with your authentic path, where a "rejection" can be seen as a sign to refine and refocus.

I began to see my signs.

PLAY WITH THE UNIVERSE

Any of the following journaling topics can shift your state of being. I say *yes* to that.

Journal to Shift Your Story

When you journal, instead of just making a list, tell a story and take your time to feel the vibrational power in your statements.

What if...

You have seen throughout the book questions that begin with *"What if..."* Asking this question is a great way to open your playfield to the infinite field of the Universe.

It is an open-ended question that activates your brain to go out to find evidence, all the proof you need to make something become a reality.

Try it for yourself right now.

What if everything was possible?

Write a page or two filled with sentences that all begin with "*What if..*" Such as:

What if I was infinitely supported?

What if I could trust myself?

What if I could choose to be free?

What if it was possible to shift my story?

What if it was easy?

What if questions do not require an answer from your conscious mind, they simply open a space of creation without the limited mind resisting. Say them out loud.

What Inspires You?

Begin to journal about all that inspires you. Inspiration shifts your vibration and attunes you to a higher state of being and possibility. Include things to look at, to wear, to do, to play, to eat, to listen to. Use your imagination to allow for the expansion of possibility and fresh inspiration. Perhaps you will find something new that surprises and delights you.

An inspiring way to give energy to this writing session is to begin a sentence with a simple: "*I love …*"

For example, "*I love blueberries. I love dancing. I love watching the ocean. I love dreaming with the stars and galaxies.*"

Keep adding to your list every time you think of something new. This activates the energy of love and inspiration every time. Add pictures if you would like.

Your Power Words and Sentences

Begin a list of power words. Write down as many words you can that carry energetic meaning for you, words that inspire, elevate, energize, soothe, relax, and calm you. Feel the essence of them. Wear their vibration.

Create power sentences with them that begin with the phrases such as "*I choose . . .*" or "*I am . . .*" For example: "*I choose freedom. I am love.*"

Pay attention when you see your words written somewhere or in reading a magazine or book. Consider it a wink from the Universe.

Keep the list going, adding to it. This keeps your brain looking for more empowerment for you.

Your Highest Vision for Three to Six Months

Shake your body. Do some light bouncing. Breathe deeply. Sit tall. Smile. Embody confidence. Imagine yourself in your highest light.

Begin writing a vision for yourself for the next three to six months. This is long enough to make a true shift and short enough for it to feel obtainable with a bit of an urgency.

Make it feel possible. Imagine with all your senses. Write as many details as possible. Increase the light and sense of excitement. Imagine yourself healthy, happy, joyous, successful, and at peace. Set your bar high.

- What are your three highest obtainable goals within three months? Six months?
- How does achieving your goals affect different areas of your life?
- Imagine how it feels to reach your goals. Describe in detail.
- Use your power words in describing your highest vision.
- What inspired action do you choose to take?
- Is there anything holding you back?

If there is anything holding you back, you will have an opportunity to clear it in the next three chapters.

Instant Shift Tip: Yes!

Feel into the word *yes*. It is an energizer. It can empower and uplift, support, and strengthen. It confirms and nods. Use it out loud and feel the Universe joining you in saying yes. Combine it with a body gesture that feels like a natural power move for you. Seal your choice and commitment with a resounding "Yes!"

To what are you saying "yes" today?

Remember to take breaks from reading and writing. Move yourself. Have a glass of water.

When you shift your body, everything shifts. Yes!

Your Wisdom Book

How is your wisdom book filling up? See how you can open it on any page and receive an inspiring message, or perhaps a sign. Continue to fill it after finishing reading this book. Make it beautiful.

- Write at least three of your power sentences in your wisdom book.
- Write at least three gratitude sentences.
- Write down anything that feels important from reading the chapter "The Universe Always Says Yes" in your wisdom book.

SIX

SHIFT YOUR STORY

When you shift, the world shifts.

W hat does shifting your story have to do with the signs of the Universe?

Everything.

Because the Universe meets you exactly where you are. It says yes to your dominant story. For you to create and co-create consciously with the Universe, you need to meet yourself where you are as well. Only through accepting where you are, can you transform your life and move to the next level.

If you feel like you are stuck in the mud and looking up to the mountain top from there, it can feel impossible to climb. No matter how much you visualize, pray, and affirm, or ask for signs, you can only move out of the mud when you acknowledge the mud. You have to be where you are first—but not necessarily for long. In fact, you will be there longer if you fight your feelings or your situation.

Perhaps being in the mud is someone's fault. Or the

circumstances are to be blamed. "Oh, poor me," you might say, "I am in the mud, I can never get out of here."

Or perhaps you did something awful that landed you in the mud. Whether you feel just a little limited or hugely stuck, it is your decision to stay in the mud or move out of the mud, and the secret to it lies in your clarity, choice, and quality of commitment.

As children, we show up with imagination and wonder. We are present to signs and dreams, and fluent in the language of the Universe. There is a moving true story of a little boy who had a newborn baby brother. He insisted that his parents allow him to talk to his baby brother alone.

The parents were naturally somewhat concerned about what he might do when he was alone with the baby, so they left the door open enough for them to hear what happened. The little boy said softly to the baby: *"Hey, as you just came from the other side, would you please remind me how it is, because I am beginning to forget."*

What Story Are You Telling?

The story you tell yourself is also the program running in your brain. Remember, your RAS filters things and events in and out of your experience based on your dominant thoughts, beliefs and habits, whether they consist of judgments and fears, or empowerment and infinite possibility. Your story is reinforced in your system through your experience.

Listen carefully to how you talk about your life, to

yourself as well as to others. Are you telling an old story that keeps limiting you, a story that doesn't allow you to create anything new? Without establishing a clear and loving, but firm and committed intention, and even intervention with a certain kind of discipline, you could easily keep looping through the same unconscious pattern of experience-story-experience-story for the rest of your life.

You give meaning to everything in your world, based on your values and needs. When you know what your values and needs are, you can consciously have them serve your highest vision, instead of a limitation. A small shift in your focus changes everything vibrationally. Are you moving toward love or avoiding rejection? Are you embracing success or hiding from failure? Are you rather bored than choose adventure? Do you allow anger to destroy your peace?

The common denominator of most limiting stories is that you blame something or someone outside of yourself that you cannot control. These stories disconnect you from the power of the present moment and its possibilities, and one way or another, make you a victim. In other words: They render you powerless When triggered, defense mechanisms may range from aggression to depression and everything in between.

When you recognize your limiting stories, and the kinds of events that trigger them, you are free to choose a more conscious and constructive way of creation and shift from reacting to responding, from following to leading, from victim to creator. When you focus your energy with clarity, conscious choice and intentionality, you train your energy system, your brain and the Universe to create a new outcome—a new story.

Let's look at the four main categories of a limiting story: limiting stories about the past, limiting stories about the future, limiting stories about yourself, and limiting stories about your circumstances.

A Limiting Story about the Past

Many of our limiting stories are based on past disappointments, frustrations, resentments, and regrets, and often planted when we were very little. While the natural inclination is to want to keep telling the story, even to put more delicious details into it, the most healing way is to embrace your inner child and have the child feel safe, heard, loved, and accepted by you now, so that you can then lead your way out of the limiting beliefs and destructive defense patterns. Whatever program or story is active in your system now, can also be healed and shifted in the now, so you may live a fresh experience in the present.

Are there stories in your mind about past events where you tend to fault, blame, or judge because it feels true? When I am working with a healing client, I often hear: *"But this isn't a story. This really happened."* I hear you. But hear me: It is not happening now. It is only a memory of what happened that keeps triggering the feeling and stopping you from being free.

"But this always happens to me," you might insist. Yes, that's the cycle of the story and the feedback that reinforces it. Every story creates a pattern and draws similar events and people into your life. But really you are interpreting everything through the filter of past pain. You give it meaning.

If you regret anything, think about it this way: You might have missed your opportunity then, how about now? Are you going to miss your opportunity right now? Choose to change your story now.

Is there anyone in your life you haven't forgiven? Do you hold resentment towards someone? As the saying goes, unforgiveness (or anger or resentment for that matter) is like taking poison and hoping for the other person to die.

Holding on to any past hurt is to keep hoping that the past will be different.

When you hold on to a past hurt, an important question to answer is: How does holding on to the story benefit you? Besides the very real rush of chemicals it releases in your brain and body, it is easy to overlook the fact that each story and action somehow benefits us. The story might gain you sympathy. It might allow you to postpone taking action that could lead to your success, keeping you "safe." Perhaps you defend your limiting story and hide behind it. Do you hide behind a story of failure, because of a fear of success? It is time to see clearly and choose differently.

Your story might serve as your "wastebasket," a place

where you can project all your pain, anger, resentment, unforgiveness, sadness, and frustration, regardless of its origin. All the while, as the defense keeps trying to keep you from having to feel the pain it actually keeps adding to your pain. It makes the pain worse, instead of relieving it.

We feed our stories vibrationally, with our feelings and emotions. When not seen and cleared, the stories founded on past hurts, disappointments, misunderstandings, violations, and such make a nest in our bodies and are easily triggered.

Pay attention when you talk with a friend, or with anyone. Are you complaining? Is a dysfunctional pattern being reinforced or released? Gossiping is one form of reinforcing your limitation. We put a lot of energy behind things like: *"Can you believe what he did?" "Outrageous." "How can anyone do that." "OMG."* Who are you using to support your disempowering story? Who supports you being stuck, angry, sad, or a victim?

You might as well use all that energy to tell yourself (and your friends) a better story. Choose to clear and shift your stories with a friend, Support each other. Empower each other. Join a master mind, hire a coach to guide you and to hold an unconditional space for you to shift, change and transform.

You can learn to recognize these patterns and pull yourself out of the story. You can teach yourself to think higher and to choose greater than your limiting story.

When we are present, we flow and respond. When we

are off, we react and interpret everything through the conditioning of the story, and we are no longer available to listen or communicate. While we might feel justified to react, we lose our bearings in the now, we try to compensate, our choices narrow down, and we find ourselves in full-blown stress mode. Over time this internal stress creates havoc in our system, weakening our immune response, digestive system, memory, sleep patterns, blood pressure, mental health, and our overall sense of wellbeing, possibility, and empowerment.

A Limiting Story about the Future

When you begin to examine your stories, you will see that stories are often intertwined. We project our past disappointments into the future because of the fear of the unknown. In fact, we fear that the past will be recreated, so in a sense we fear what we think we know. As discussed before, we are wired, by our past experiences, to prepare for the worst.

What if, instead, we began now to prepare for the best?

"But then it will be a disaster if it doesn't work out. I will be disappointed again," someone might say. That comment just reveals a vibrational state of fear and worry. It is natural to defend a limitation, because it feels familiar and even "safe."

When you "protect" yourself from any future disappointments, or disasters, you are also easily "protecting" yourself from wonderful events from happening. Any fear projected into the future blocks you from experiencing your authentic flow, happiness, creativity and growth.

If you are worried and anxious about the future or the unknown, remind yourself that this is just a part of you. See if you can learn to accept and embrace the aspect of you that is afraid, insecure or fearful – or angry, resentful and frustrated. So that you don't identify or define yourself through your triggered wounds, and that the defensive reactions do not run your life.

When we pull ourselves out of the fear-based story, we are free to create a new expanded vision. We learn to follow the invitation of the future possibility rather than being trapped in a limiting story.

As the saying goes: *The best way to control your future is to create it.*

A Limiting Story about Yourself

Who are you? Who do you want to be?

The limiting story of self can be sneaky. We often identify with this type of story so much that we think it is the truth and there is nothing we can do about it. But a story is only true if you believe it. You may find yourself in situations that are hard and feel hopeless. But even then, you have a choice of your thoughts and the meaning you give them.

If Victor Frankl can find meaning enough to survive holocaust, or if Nick Santonastasso can become a motivational coach and a prize-winning bodybuilder with one arm and no legs, so can you choose an empowering mindset over any limitation.

Find stories of people who have overcome the "mission impossible." There are so many success stories proving that, yes, you can heal, you can prosper, you can change, you can learn, you can grow, or you can find love, against all odds. You name it. However, if you have a belief that contradicts any such possibility for you, it is important to recognize it, so that you don't remain its prisoner.

Do you identify any feelings, beliefs, or patterns that put you down? Do you, for instance, ever say things like "*I should already have succeeded? By this age I should be married?*" There is often a "should" or "should have" in these limiting stories.

The story can also be: "*If I were younger, thinner, richer, more beautiful, more educated, then I could . . .*" or "*I'm too old, it's too late.*" In this way, your story puts conditions on your happiness. Look for anything that gives you an excuse for why you can't be, have or do what you desire.

Why do we hold on to stories that keep us small? By now we understand how the story keeps being recycled through everything in our experience. When we see proof for our limiting story, we think it must be true.

It might feel comfortable to hide behind a limitation. We might nurture the limitation, and think we are nurturing and healing the wound. Look for any comfortable, wise sounding explanation for why you are not moving ahead, taking action, choosing or changing. How is the story serving you? Is it safer to be stuck? Is it easier to stay with what feels familiar than to commit to your dream? Is it easier to hide behind anger or sadness than it is to have courage to love?

A Limiting Story about Circumstances

Do you feel that if the circumstances were different you could be happy? If someone else changed their behavior? If they understood you better? If you had more money? If you had a family, or if you didn't have a family? These are stories of projection, where something out there is preventing you from being happy.

This type of story leads to not taking responsibility for your own well-being and instead blaming your circumstances and then trying to change, fix, or control others. This story easily mixes with the limiting past stories and leads to gossiping, criticizing, and judging others. We get defensive and judge ourselves.

We already know that we think 60,000–70,000 thoughts every day, and about 90 percent of them are exactly the same thoughts as the day before. We don't even notice it. If our thoughts are always basically the same, and they create emotional reactions, then the emotions subsequently feed the thoughts again, and the loop keeps going on until you stop the cycle.

Perhaps you are saying, *"I'm doing everything I can to change my circumstances and the circumstances are not changing."* But are you really? It might feel like you are making a huge effort, because you tell the story with such dedication. The energy of resistance is very dense, and you feel you are working so hard. You actually are, but you cannot force your way through it. You cannot create something different by pushing against the energy you want to change. Rather, you must change your energy. Interrupt the pattern. When you change your vibration, everything changes.

You might say: *"But I want to have goals and take action! There has to be something I can actually do."* Dear one, I hear you, but unless you shift your vibration first and commit with crystalline clarity to thinking in a new way, your actions will result in the same circumstances as before. Or, you might have a brilliant idea, but if you are not a vibrational match, you talk yourself out of it. Tend to your vibration first, so that you don't create on the level of your doubts and fears.

By default, reality is relative. It is based on interpretations, beliefs, definitions, opinions, judgments, and such. Much of it is adopted, learned, repeated, and recycled from family, friends, and the collective consciousness. When we see the world through the eyes of limitation, limitation is reflected right back to us. We always find proof for what we want to see, or for what our beliefs dictate us to see.

This is not only the law of attraction; it is what we know through neuroscience.

You are the creator and the creation, the source and substance of your reality. No matter what your circumstances are, you do have a choice about who you are. Everything changes when you choose.

If you are feeling like a victim or imagine that you are powerless to control your situation, or you are cycling through a negative thought pattern of any kind that is limiting your life, then these feelings don't allow the flow of consciousness at the level of love, caring, or wellbeing.

It is important to note that being a victim is not only when you feel sad, weak, or like "poor me," but equally when you are angry, resentful or frustrated because of someone or something outside of yourself. You might get some relief from blaming others, the past, or your circumstances, but blame won't give you your power back, nor can it elevate your consciousness so that you are able to create something new and different in the future.

Ask yourself: "Who would I be without this story?"

How to Shift Your Story

You are more space than matter. Scientifically 99.9999999999999 percent of every atom is empty space. Think about it. Quite amazing. Those atoms form molecules that represent the form known as you. Your physical body only seems solid. Each time you move, your molecules rearrange themselves in the Universe, in the field of possibility and potentiality, to look like you. What if you allowed the molecules to reorganize to reflect the highest vision for yourself?

To choose and commit to a new story does not have to

be hard, but it might not always be easy, because your mind will try to trick you to think it is hard, complicated, or even not possible. You mind will want to seduce you back to the old. In fact, as with any change, you need to be willing to be comfortable with being uncomfortable for a moment. However, it is very empowering to show your mind your new choice from the perspective of higher consciousness.

Don't use your will power to fight yourself through thick and thin, but use it to create clarity of thought, to refocus your energy, to make conscious choices, and most importantly to keep your commitment. You show your mind who's the leader. You retrain it to focus in a new story. Whenever you have a looping thought, ask yourself: *"Who's thinking these thoughts in my head?"* Choose any of the instant shift techniques to stop, to shake it off, to snap out of it, to elevate your vibration, to reset. Do it right away to interrupt the limiting story and to recondition yourself.

To begin shifting any story, do an inventory to see what authentically serves you. Look at your thoughts and dominant beliefs that direct your life, and ask yourself again: *"Does this make me feel heavy or light? Does my energy go up or down? Do I feel restricted or expanded?"* Follow expanded, up, light and lightness. Then, stop engaging with the rest of it. Interrupt the pattern. Change your breath, posture, thoughts and energy.

You might say, *"I don't know what I'm supposed to do. I don't know my authentic calling or purpose,"* or *"I know what I want, but not know how to get there."* I promise you, once you focus and refocus your thoughts and feelings, once you stop telling your disempowering story, you won't have to search for your calling. Once you know how to play with the Universe and how to elevate your vibration in the now, your options appear. You no longer are chasing your dream, or figuring out your purpose. You teach yourself to choose it with crystalline clarity and steadfast commitment without looking back, then when you take action, it will be inspired action. You raise the bar. You show up with focus and commitment.

In fact, when you choose to keep your momentum going by tending to your vibration and honoring your commitment every day, you will become a magnet to goodness, grace, abundance, love, and to anything that represents the essence of your dreams. Release everything that stands in the way to the recycling center of the Universe.

Become a Space of Clarity

Make it a habit to pause every now then throughout your day and breathe for grounding and connection: earth, light, heart. Be present with nothing to figure out, fix, or do, nowhere to go, no role to play, no pressure to be anything.

Imagine yourself in your highest light. See yourself happy, fulfilled, and at peace. Expand that vision some more. Allow your body to reflect that. Embody yourself in your highest light. Use powerful "What if" and "How would it feel" questions to open the field of possibility for you.

"Wear" the energy of magic and miracles. Imagine.

For our purposes, clarity is a vibrationally clear space, a sparkling clear space of the infinite now. A space of possibility and potentiality, free of confusion, doubt, fear, resentment, regret, "not possible," "not good enough," and other limiting stories. Any limitation permits the creative consciousness of the Universe to support you only on that level. Raise and elevate the vibration first, in order to allow your matrix of possibility to open and expand to the higher consciousness, to all that is, to where miracles, healing, and manifestation happen all the time.

Clarity is a state of being. It is the infinite now, the still point between inbreath and outbreath, where everything is possible. It is your pure presence without a story, the energetic womb of creation, from where you receive all the answers and guidance you need, where you trust your interpretation of signs. Clarity is a space of surrender, where you let go of your need to control, where you allow to be surprised by the unknown. To become the space of clarity, leave your baggage at the door. Shake your body if you need to. Reclaim your energy. Say "Yes" to yourself. Allow a deep loving breath, straighten your spine, see yourself in your highest light, and say: *I am ready to choose and commit. Show me the way.*

Choose Consciously

Within the space of clarity, you begin to see choices. The more you elevate your vibration, the clearer you become, the more you see what limits you and what else is possible. First: Choose to know yourself. Choose to honor yourself. Choose to focus your energy and attention with crystalline clarity into seeing yourself in your highest light always. Choose to be on your side. Choose your truth, path, and power. Choose to trust yourself, your guidance, and the Universe.

Choice is a clear intention, an announcement to your brain and a signal to the Universe that you mean business, you are in. You either choose or you don't. There are no two ways about it. A choice doesn't leave you hanging, it takes you by the hand and guides you.

A conscious choice leads you to a new life, one step at a time. You don't have to force your way to your new life; it comes to you. Don't get me wrong, you will still take gigantic, massive action, but it comes from your inner guidance, not from what you think you *should* do. The signs will show up. You are guided to take inspired action. But you have to choose first.

Instead of hoping, wishing, or trying, you do what?

You choose.

When you learn to elevate your vibration first and bring your choices to the space of clarity, it allows the highest level of consciousness of the Universe to move through to support your choice.

You supercharge yourself and the Universe into motion for creation, fulfillment, and manifestation.

Commitment: Your Secret Power

Choice and commitment must go together. Without commitment your choice loses its momentum and dissipates. Where choosing announces your intention to the Universe and sets the manifestation in motion, your commitment keeps the momentum going.

Your commitment is the Excalibur to help you win the battle, to keep your vibration high and to ensure you are a vibrational match to the most outstanding option in your matrix of possibility. It means not only understanding how the principles of shifting work, but also being willing to do whatever it takes to keep your commitment to the new highest vision of yourself and your life. When you commit, your life changes. Everything in your life now begins to be filtered according to your new choice and commitment. You create a new conditioning.

When you are energetically elevated, present and alive in the now, and when you imagine with gratitude and unwavering focus your new life as if it were already your reality, the higher consciousness of the Universe floods in with full support. As you elevate energetically, the support elevates exponentially.

Your mind will try to convince you that the 70,000 old thoughts are just fine. The mind might need proof that the change or shift is working. It is like backseat passengers asking their driver, *"Are we there yet? How much longer? Is this working?"*

Your mind might even say: *"This is not working. It is not worth it. You have tried before."* When we begin to look for proof in the middle of transformation or creation, we disrupt the flow of the process and slip back towards the old story, towards fears and doubts. When we say, *"I can't,"* our brain doesn't even begin to find solutions.

Instead, disrupt the backseat driver and keep training your mind and body to stay focused. If you begin telling the old story, even in your head, no matter how delicious it might feel, stop immediately, even in the middle of a sentence. Shake it off.

Choose and commit.

Again, keep in mind: Where attention goes, energy flows.

The Universe responds on the level of your vibration. Your signs will get clearer, stronger, and louder. Your signs shift as you shift.

PLAY WITH THE UNIVERSE

What follows first is a meditation to hold space for your inner child. Then we dig deep into recognizing any limiting story to turn it around and to be free to choose a new story. Are you willing to choose and to commit?

Say "yes!" if you are.

An Inner Child Meditation: You Are a Child of the Universe

Because most of our fears and limiting stories have their roots in our childhood, it is powerful to learn to hold, nurture and love our inner child instead of rejecting or ignoring him or her. Then we can be whole and integrated here and now.

Read the meditations slowly, pausing as you need, feeling into the space you create in your imagination.

As it says in the meditation, receive and be received. If you would like to listen to it, you may find this meditation on my website or my YouTube channel as my gift to you (see Resources for more details).

Thank you for being here, thank you for being you and for trusting your own guidance.

Breathe and relax.

Allow a moment to feel the energy of the earth, tune in to it. Inhale the livingness of the earth. You are infinitely connected to its intelligence, to its web of nurturing growth and healing.

Receive and be received.

Imagine a beautiful light coming down like a soft rain or mist from the Universe, from the heavens. This healing light embraces you and fills you, activating every atom of your energy field. Imagine it almost tickling you, yes, and gently reminding you that you are a beautiful child of the Universe.

Now imagine yourself, like a child would imagine it, in a beautiful temple of divine light and infinite love. It feels safe and you feel at peace.

Feel the gentle presence of guides and angels, beings of the highest light. Perhaps you can see them surrounding you, supporting you, beaming their loving light on you.

How does it feel?

How do you see yourself in this gentle healing light?

Imagine that you sit down in the middle of this temple, any place that feels comfortable for you.

Now, looking towards the entrance, you see a child there.

It is you as a little child.

Invite the little you to sit with you, allowing him or her to be any age.

As you open your arms, say to the child: "May I hold you?"

Honor the child, hold the child, and rock him or her gently.

Look the child deeply in the eyes and say: "I see you. I love you. Thank you for being you."

As the child relaxes in your arms, ask him or her to show you one event, occurring at any age, that is still bothering him or her in some way, an event where the child felt hurt, wronged, judged, blamed, or shamed in any way.

Hold space for the child as the angels and guides hold space for both of you.

Witness as the child shows you in words, in pictures, in sensations. Like you're watching a movie of the memory.

It is the child's version of events. There's no need to explain, no need to justify, no need to clarify or correct.

Have pure love and acceptance for the child.

When the child finishes with his or her story, hold the child and rock him or her gently.

Say, "I feel you. I know."

Look the child deeply in the eyes and say, "I see you. I love you. I'm so sorry for what you had to go through. I'm so sorry that you carried this within you all this time."

Ask the child if she or he would be willing now to let go of this hurt.

Communicate to the child that you are right here, that she or he is not alone.

Feel the guides and angels right there with you.

You are not alone. You are never alone.

Imagine the child lifting his or her hands in a cup holding a stone. This stone represents the event in question. The stone itself is not good or bad; it just represents the event that took place.

What color is this stone?

What size is this stone?

As the child holds the stone, now hold the child's hand, so that you are holding the stone together. Imagine all the angels and guides holding space around you, as you and the child lift your hands up, up, up, releasing the stone into the light, into the light, into the light. Letting go now, letting go now, letting go now.

It floats up.

And you see it dissolving into golden light of healing with all its energies and energetics of the hurt from this time and all other times, from this dimension and all other dimensions, known or unknown, with all the information and data of what has kept the wound open and the story active in your system.

There it goes. It's gone. It's gone. It's gone.

Look the child deep in the eyes and say, "I see you. Thank you for being so brave today. I am right here with you. I am so proud of you. I will never abandon you. I listen to you. I believe you. I honor you. I support you. I keep you safe."

Feel the joy bubbling in the child.

In return for your support, the child gives you magic, creativity, curiosity, wonder, courage, joy, and innocence.

She or he is now the wonder child, the magic child. Together you can bring so much into this world.

You are both held in the sacredness by the beings of the highest light. They celebrate this moment of freedom and truth with you.

You are a beautiful powerful child of the Universe, of the divine light. Thank you for being here. Thank you for being you and for trusting your guidance.

Journal to Shift Your Story

As always, it is good to journal on your meditation and write down any details or insights that are meaningful to you.

Then I invite you to look at any limiting beliefs, because what you see it clearly, you can choose to interrupt. Our limiting stories keep us from seeing the truth, which very often is the exact opposite of the limitation.

This is your opportunity to shift a "no" to "yes," or move "not good enough" to "more than enough" through "good, great and excellent" to "extraordinary, outstanding and unstoppable." Or whatever you choose to shift now. Instead of "trying, hoping and wishing," you begin choosing and deciding.

It is time to stop being a victim of your own beliefs and stories. Here, I invite you to be honest with yourself without judgment, and choose to step into your truth, power and potential.

Breathe.

Smile.

Your Inner Child

After reading the meditation with vivid imagination or listening to it as a guided meditation, journal about your experience with your inner child.

- What age was she or he, who showed up today?
- How did the event from the past feel from the child's perspective?
- How did it feel from your perspective?
- Do you feel a difference in your relationship to your inner child?
- What is possible for you with your magic child?

Your Old Limiting Stories of the Past, Future, Yourself, and Your Circumstances

When you understand what limits you, you can neutralize and shift it. Look for any story or belief that is holding you back in any way, or that makes you small, or where you say: "*I can't.*"

Look for where you feel that you are powerless, hopeless, confused, sad, angry or frustrated.

Choose to shift, change and transform them now.

Shift Your Limiting Story of the Past

Identify anything in your past that keeps you from being free and happy in the now.

When a story is active, it keeps triggering you and disempowering you.

Journal on each of the following questions.

- What is your most limiting story or belief from the past? If there are more than one that comes to mind, journal on each one.
- How does it make you feel?
- What triggers the story?
- What is your number one go-to emotion that is triggered by a limiting story from the past?
- How has this story affected different areas of your life?
- Is there anyone to forgive? Yourself? Someone else?
- What choices can you make today to shift the story?
- What action can you take to neutralize the trigger?

Change Your Past

Think of any event from your past that you would have liked to be different. Write it down, not as it happened, but as you would have wanted it to happen, as if it actually happened so.

Be a storyteller. Use all your imagination to create a new happy memory. Make it so rich in detail that reading it makes you believe in it as if it was a real memory. This can be very powerful, so begin with a memory that doesn't have a huge emotional charge.

Shift Your Limiting Story of the Future

Identify any story on worrying about the future. Look for beliefs such as: "*I already know what will happen,*" or "*It will not work,"* or *"Why try,"* or fears of the unknown or paths not chosen because of the fear of making the wrong choice.

- What are your limiting stories about the future?
- Do you recognize limiting certainties or beliefs you know "for sure" about the future?
- What are your greatest fears about the future?
- What triggers the stories, beliefs or fears?
- What is your number one go-to emotion that is triggered by a limiting story?
- Where have you learned from these stories? Whose stories are they?
- How does each of them limit your life?
- How could you interrupt the pattern of the triggers?
- With what can you replace these stories?

Good News and Miracles: An Interview with the Future

Commit to collecting miracle stories, good news, and proof of the impossible. Commit to being a miracle story, teaching by example, and telling your own story of healing, change or empowerment. Show the world that miracles are within everyone's reach. Then, imagine being the subject of a news story or an interview a few months or years into the future.

From the perspective of your future, explore also *why* you succeeded. What was the driving force for you to choose to make the shift and transform your life? Why did you "have to" do it? Your *why* gives you clarity, meaning and commitment, so that your *how* can begin to show up.

Write out an interview on how you began to shift your story and to see new signs. Tell your personal story of choice, commitment, and transformation. Imagine empowering others with your story, perhaps even hundreds, thousands, or millions of people by saying: *"If I can do this, you can too."*

Shift Your Limiting Story of Yourself

Identify any story where you put yourself down, beat yourself up, judge yourself or compare yourself to others. Such as: Not good enough, not worthy, not lovable, not smart enough, shame, guilt, and so on.

- What is your dominant limiting belief or story about yourself? You are of course welcome to explore more than one.
- What triggers the story?
- What is your number one go-to emotion that is triggered by a limiting story of yourself?
- Do you beat yourself up verbally? Either in your thoughts or even out loud? What do you say?
- Do you encourage yourself verbally? Either in your thoughts or out loud?
- Which one comes easier criticizing or praising?
- Who do you use to support your story?
- What limiting story are you willing to shift today?
- What do you fear the most in your personal life?
- How is the fear serving you? Is it keeping you safe?

- What does the fear or limitation reveal on the opposite side? What could you choose instead of the fear? What is the truth on the other side?
- How would your life change if you let go of the fears and beliefs that limit you?

A Love Letter to Yourself

Write a love letter to yourself from your higher self. Be free to write anything you would need to hear. As always, use your imagination and creativity, but if you need inspiration, begin with expressions like (completing the sentence with what is true for you):

- *"I love you because..."*
- *"Thank you for being so..."*
- *"I'm so proud of you because..."*
- *"I will always remember how you..."* (only something you admire and love)
- *"It makes me so happy that...*
- *"You don't have to worry, because I..."*
- *"You can trust that..."*
- *"I know, you can..."*

Shift Your Limiting Story of the Circumstances

Identify any story where you project your unhappiness on others or on your circumstances in general. Stories of projecting blame sound like: *"If they understood, then..."* or *"If I had more money, then..."*

Write about any story where you feel you are trapped

and helpless and where your limitation is someone else's fault or due to dire circumstances.

- What is your top limiting story of blaming the circumstances? If there are more stories, write about each one.
- How does is make you feel?
- What is your number one go-to emotion that is triggered by a limiting story?
- By now, do you see any pattern in your number one go-to emotion? See your answers in the previous prompts. When you shift this one emotion, your whole story shifts.
- How does it serve you to blame something outside of you?
- What triggers the projection?
- Would you be willing to take responsibility of your own life? How would your life change if you shifted this story?
- What beliefs would you have to let go to release the story?
- Who would you be without this story?
- What action are you willing to take today to let go of this limiting story?

Instant Shift Tip: A Playdate

Plan a playdate with your inner child. Tune in and ask what she or he would like to do with you. Be playful and creative. Use your imagination. See with the eyes of curiosity. Explore innocence and joy. You might want to commit to a playdate at least once a week.

Your Wisdom Book

Find quotes from inspiring people based on their powerful stories of transformation and resilience. We often see only their success after any hardship and assume it has always been easy for them.

- Find stories of people who were told they are not going to succeed or amount to anything, but they turned it around and became an outstanding success in their chosen field.
- Find stories of people who grew up poor or lost everything, and against all odds chose to not let their limiting story stop them from becoming a leader and a philanthropist.
- Find stories of people who were told they had no hope of healing and they did heal completely.
- Write three statements of gratitude and appreciation in each of the following categories: your past, yourself, people in your life and your current circumstances.

SEVEN

TAP YOUR WAY TO EMOTIONAL FREEDOM

I choose to love, honor and accept myself deeply and completely as I am.

I f I had to name one tool to work on stuck feelings or limiting emotions, it would be the emotional freedom technique (EFT), also known as tapping. EFT is simple to do and anyone can learn it, yet it is very powerful for neutralizing unwanted emotions. EFT can also help you in shifting a painful or limiting story, so that you may let your heart soften and you may embrace yourself with kindness and compassion.

The origins of this technique go all the way back to ancient China because it uses some of the same meridian points that are used in acupuncture. The form of tapping we do now originated with the groundbreaking work of psychologist Roger Callahan, Ph.D., who created a system of tapping meridian end points to treat his clients, which he called thought field therapy. Later, one of his students,

Gary Craig, a performance coach, created a system of an easy sequence of the tapping points, which helped popularize tapping.

There are many wonderful videos on the internet to tap with on every topic you can think of. You will find videos on my website and YouTube channel as well. While every practitioner's approach to tapping is endowed with the personal flavor of their teaching and elements of their expertise, the principles of tapping remain the same: You name a feeling or emotion you want to neutralize. Then, tapping gently with your fingers on various meridian points, you make affirmative statements out loud. The tapping activates your neurological system to release the emotional charge named and allows space for reprograming, ultimately bringing your system to homeostasis and neutrality.

This process allows you to take back your power and gives you freedom to see the world through a neutral space of clarity and love, rather than the limited point of view of the trapped emotion. That being said, you don't necessarily have to have a "problem" of a limited emotion to use tapping, you can also tap for appreciation and elevation, to strengthen and to expand the good vibes.

I have personally seen some amazing results with EFT in neutralizing limiting, even paralyzing emotions, both for myself and my clients, who include war veterans, assault victims, terminally ill people, people dealing with betrayal, separation or grief, and others coping with intense, highly charged emotions that seem impossible to overcome. I have had clients who systematically tapped on everything we could think of and their lives cleared up in dramatic and surprising ways.

While you can get support and security from working with a practitioner, you can perfectly well do tapping by yourself. However, if you feel unsafe in any way in general, or your emotions feel unbearable or intolerable, please always seek professional help. Ask the Universe for guidance in finding the perfect professional support for you.

A powerful healing can take place when you learn to love yourself and accept yourself exactly as you are, especially the parts that feel the most undeserving of love or the most unacceptable. Those wounded parts have already felt rejected, not loved, not worthy, or not good enough. What if you could embrace them now instead? Allow each part of you to integrate into the wholeness of who you are. Teach all the parts of you that it is safe to love.

The idea is to learn to love and accept ourselves exactly as we are, not after something changes or something has been fixed. That is why the beginning statement is: *Even though I feel* [fill in your feeling], *I love and accept myself exactly as I am.* Sometimes it is hard to say, "I love myself." In that case, go easy on yourself and say phrase such as:

- *"I am willing to learn to love myself."*
- *"I am willing to learn to accept, honor and value myself exactly as I am."*

- *"I choose to learn to love myself deeply and completely."*
- *"I choose to learn to accept, honor and value myself deeply and completely exactly as I am."*

Here follows the basic outline, so that if you like, you may begin right away, or skip it for now and come back to it at any time you need it.

You will find EFT instruction videos on my website (see Resources for details).

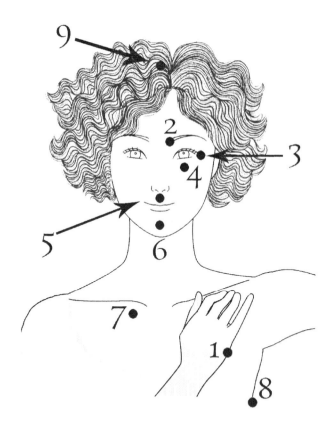

After the tapping points and the description of how to do the technique, there are ideas for what to use it. I have also included ideas for tapping to celebrate, appreciate, strengthen, and expand an already clear and high-vibrating space.

The Tapping Points

There are nine tapping points, which are gently tapped with two or three fingertips in the same sequence.

Tapping with either hand or on either side is fine.

Perform tapping in the following sequence.

1. **Beginning point: The Karate Chop Point.** This is the chubby area on the side of your hand under your pinky, where you would imagine breaking a board with a karate chop. Thus, the name. This point is only used in the beginning of each set of sequence.
2. **Inner Corner of the Eyebrow.** You may tap on either eyebrow or both eyebrows if you like.
3. **Outer Corner of the Eye.** Just where the bone is.
4. **Under the Eye.** Again, you will feel a bone there.
5. **Under the Nose.**
6. **Chin.** On the front side below the lower lip.
7. **Under the Clavicle** (collar bone).
8. **Under the Arm.** On the side of the body below the armpit, where a woman would have her bra.
9. **On Top of the Head.**

How to Do Tapping

As said, tapping with either hand or on either side is fine. You say one sentence per point. Once you begin, the tapping continues throughout. You may tap six times, if the sentence is short, or you may tap twenty times or more if the sentence is longer or you think for a moment what to say. The idea is to keep the tapping going, not to count how many times you tap.

Name a Limiting Feeling or Emotion

Name a feeling that has a limiting emotional charge for you that you would like to neutralize and integrate into peace, harmony, and love. It is most powerful to concentrate on one feeling or emotion at a time.

Notice the Intensity of the Feeling or Emotion

On a scale from 1–10 what is the emotional charge or intensity on that feeling for you at this time. Ten being very intense and one almost nothing. What you measure, improves.

Begin Tapping the Karate Chop Point

Begin gentle rhythmic tapping on the Karate Chop Point, say: *"I take full responsibility for my wellbeing."*

The basic structure of the beginning statement is: *Even though I feel* [fill in your feeling], *I love and accept myself exactly as I am.*

My favorite is to use the words "choose" and also "honor" in the beginning statement. Let's say you wish to neutralize "Worry."

Keep it simple. Continue tapping on the Karate Chop Point and say the beginning statement three times: *"Even though I feel worried, I* **choose** *to love, honor and accept myself deeply and completely as I am."* Or you may want to say: *"Even though I feel worried,* **I choose to learn** *to love, honor and accept myself deeply and completely as I am."*

Once you begin to flow with it you may play with the wording, but I recommend keeping the basic structure of loving and accepting yourself no matter how you feel.

Tapping on Points 2–9: You Say It as It Is

In the first rounds, you can just say it like it feels in the moment. Keep talking while you tap your way through the points. Keep the sentences short. One sentence per point works well. You tap the frustration and limiting stuff out. If possible, talk out loud. You are not affirming it; you are releasing it. This allows the limiting program to move and create space for the new.

Keep the gentle tapping going, move to the next point and keep tapping even when you are looking for words for the next thing to say.

You are welcome to tap on the example here:

Inner corner of the eyebrow: *"All this worry."*

Outer corner of the eye: *"I am worried."*

Under the eye: *"I can't stop worrying."*

Under the nose: *"I hate to worry."*

Chin: *"I don't know what to do about the worry."*

Under the collar bone: *"I don't want to be like this."*

Under arm: *"This will never stop."*

Top of the head: *"I am tired of worrying."*

Keep going, again **inner corner of the eyebrow:** *"Enough already."*

Outer corner of the eye: *"I don't like myself when I worry."*

Continue tapping as long as you feel you have said it all. One point, one sentence.

Here are some more examples: *"I want to be happy. It is so-and-so's fault that I worry. They make me worry. They should not make me worry. I worry. I can't stop it. Whose worrying in my head? Why can't I stop it? I just can't. It is my destiny to worry. It will never stop. I am like this. I worry too much."*

You get the point. In this space, you allow even the most obvious victim stuff to be said out loud. You don't "try" to understand and analyze. Allow yourself to say things you would not say otherwise. Tap it out of your system. Let it go. If you don't know what to say, you can just repeat: *"All this worry,"* on each point. It still works.

Allow a Deep Breath and Reassess the Intensity of the Feeling or Emotion

After a few rounds through, you are ready to stop tapping for a moment. Breathe in slowly through your nose, and then exhale through your mouth while making the sound *"Aaahhh."* You may also want to do a gentle body shake to release further.

Feel into the emotional charge. See if the number has come down on the scale of 1–10. See also if anything else comes up for you. Make a note of this to work on after you are done with the feeling or emotion you are currently tapping for.

Tap in the Same Sequence Again

If the emotional charge is still above 5, continue tapping the same way. Use your own intuition on this. If you assessed and noticed that you got considerable relief from the first round of tapping and the number of the charge is now under 5, you may begin to tap with a possibility of a total relief and a new story.

Always begin the gentle rhythmic tapping with the Karate Chop Point. In this case, where you are working on "Worry," say: *"Even though I still feel a bit worried, I choose to love, honor, and accept myself deeply and completely as I am."*

Again, tapping on the rest of the points, saying one sentence per point.

You are welcome to tap on the example here.

Inner corner of the eyebrow: *"I'm still a little worried."*
Outer corner of the eye: *"But it doesn't worry me as much."*
Under the eye: *"What if I could let it go?"*
Under the nose: *"What if I could be free?"*
Chin: *"I choose to let it go."*
Under the collar bone: *"I choose to let it go a little more."*

Under arm: *"Oh, that feels good."*
Top of the head: *"I like it."*
Inner corner of the eyebrow: *"I know I can let it go."*
Outer corner of the eye: *I'm willing to let it go."*
Under the eye: *"I let go of any and all worry now."*
Under the nose: *"I release it."*
Chin: *"I choose to let it go."*

Keep tapping, keep going through the points: *"I choose to be free. I choose to allow myself to trust that freedom. I am willing to accept my feelings and learn to trust. I am willing to learn to love myself so I can trust. I love how trusting feels. I think I can do this. I choose to trust. I choose to love myself. I choose to accept myself totally and completely. I commit to loving and accepting myself. I commit to trusting. I choose to commit to trusting. I trust. I am trust. I am freedom. I am love. I am."*

End with a deep loving breath and a moment of gratitude.

Trust the process.

Check where you are again intensity-wise on the scale from 1–10. You can keep going with the sequence as long as you feel you need to or check back the next day.

Tapping for Emotional Freedom

In pursuit of freedom, here are some ideas of what you can tap for to release. Tap for anything that has come up for you in the journaling.

- Limiting emotions like shame, blame, abandonment, guilt, and fear.

- Limiting beliefs, patterns of thought, judgments.
- Anything that makes you angry or frustrated.
- Anyone that makes you angry, sad, irritated.
- Forgiveness, or the difficulty of it.
- Any part of yourself that you've rejected.
- Issues in your relationships with your spouse, children, parents, siblings, friends and even strangers.
- Issues related to money, work, and success.
- Your body image, health, and sexuality.
- Anything that makes you feel smaller or stuck.

Tapping for Appreciation and Elevation

Tapping can amplify any positive emotions without having to feel emotionally limited. It can help reinforce your new elevated vision. Some of the journaling you have done can give you useful insights now.

Here are some ideas that may serve either as your new programming after doing a purging round of tapping, or by themselves without any purging, just to appreciate, celebrate and elevate.

Here you don't need to check the intensity of the emotional charge.

The beginning statement would also reinforce and support: *I choose to love, honor and accept myself exactly as I am.*

Choose any or all of the following to tap for:

- Gratitude. Say: *"I am grateful for ..."*
- Solutions and new possibilities. Say: *"What if ..."*

- Personal power. Say: *"I choose . . ."* and *" I love . . ."* and *"I commit to . . ."*
- Affirmation. Say: *"Yes!"* Examples: *"I choose love myself. Yes! I am radiantly healthy. Yes! I love money and money loves me. Yes!"*
- Use your power statements and words.
- Have fun creating as many ways to tap for empowerment as possible.
- Write scripts for your tapping in your journal.

EIGHT

TELL A BETTER STORY OF LOVE, MONEY, HEALTH, AND WORLD PEACE

*When your reaction is to love less, choose consciously
to love more. Respond instead of reacting.
Lead instead of following.*

I f you thought you could skip directly to this chapter to
tell a better story about anything in your life and be
done with it, you will be disappointed. But if you have done
any of the exploration, you know now how to program your
mind and body so that the Universe can say yes to you and
higher consciousness can flow in.

In the neutral space of the Universe, love is the glue that
keeps everything together. In the space of clarity of the
present moment, where all creation is possible, love is the
highest essence and the most potent magic. It is the
greatest power to hold your highest dreams and visions and

to heal any and all wounds of all time and space.

Love is also perhaps the world's most misused word, in all languages—at least all those I know. We need to rescue and redeem it from total inflation, not only for love's sake, but also for ours, so that we can be whole again. As the word *love* continues to be used in so many contexts very far from the actual vibration of love, it is easy to lose the clarity of its meaning and the immensity of its transformational and healing power.

The Love of Your Life: You

We know intellectually how important it is to love ourselves. This sounds like a brilliant idea, but what does it really mean? Unfortunately, many of us are conditioned to think self-love equals being selfish. Very few of us grew up having a perfectly healthy and balanced self-esteem, or could count on the encouragement and support needed to spread our wings and blossom in life. Usually when someone says, *"You are selfish,"* it means you don't act or behave the way they would like you to.

Often since childhood, we have heard the word *love* used in contexts where there is no vibration of love to match it. Even threats have been made in the name of "love." Some serious and some more lighthearted, nevertheless all pattern-forming for a child who is not yet able to discern.

Authentic self-love is necessary for you to be able reclaim your authentic power and to love others or the world. Only through loving yourself will you be able to receive and feel worthy. Self-love is the basis for the balance, harmony, peace, and freedom you need to live your purpose. Love is not dramatic. It doesn't ask you to be a martyr or a victim. We all have witnessed someone at some point saying something like, *"I do everything for you because I love you,"* in a sacrificing way. Or *"How many times do I have to tell you that I love you?"* in an irritated voice. Or give a punishment in the name of love. We learn the romantic story of someone completing us. This has nothing to do with love. It is the perfect codependent relationship set-up. This pattern is usually picked at a young age when we are children.

Love is a neutral energy that accepts you as you are. No conditions, no judgment, no good or bad. No reward or punishment. You don't have to "try" to be worth it. It is always there for you. It receives you with open arms every time, all the time.

When we anchor unconditional love into our everyday human existence, it anchors us to our truth and power. While we invite and embrace the heights of inspiration and consciousness, our commitment to ourselves is shown in the quality of small, practical, everyday moments.

Love doesn't always come in the form of a human being that you would like—but in one form or another, love is present for you to receive. That is why it is called *unconditional love.* As we said before, receive it from where it is, rather than suffer trying to get it from where it is not. There is nothing to deserve. Love is. Love loves. Allow it.

Forgiveness Is an Act of Self-Love

One of the most powerful, painful blocks is not being able to, or not wanting to forgive. It holds you in an ugly prison, keeping love and redemption out of reach for you.

Gently see if you are being hurt by holding on to any unforgiveness. It makes you interpret everything through that the lens of wounded defense. It is hard, if not impossible, to receive love or resolution when you feel hurt or angry. You cannot accept it or trust it. Holding on to resentment hurts you, not the person you think. The poison you are taking will kill you, not them.

We might not always get an opportunity for completion with the actual people in a story of hurt and resentment, but sometimes when we do, we turn it down. It often feels safer to hold on to the resentment than to drop it.

A story of being wronged or injured can feel like part of your identity. Nonetheless, the completion is always fully available right here for you to choose, so that healing can take place. Forgiveness is an act of self-love. It doesn't mean you agree on what happened, it doesn't mean you have to ever like the person involved. It doesn't mean you have to come together physically with the person to forgive, but it does mean you choose yourself over the painful story.

Forgiveness means you choose to be free of the burden and be at peace in your heart.

It means you choose love over resentment. You forgive, because *you* deserve it.

Healthy Boundaries

Sometimes we want to understand or help others endlessly to the point of disrespecting ourselves. I personally have been in situations where I was totally walked over because I thought it should be common sense to respect other people.

After all, any conflict comes from a conflict of beliefs, values, and point of views. We make rules and create assumptions based on what we believe is true. And then those rules clash or are misunderstood, or expected to be the same for everyone. It always serves to communicate with clarity and to stand in your truth and integrity in any given situation.

What is important to you, might be low on the list with someone else. They would not know how important it is, unless you tell them. And even then, they might not remember to honor it every time, which doesn't mean they don't love or respect you.

This relates right back to the issue of loving yourself and honoring your needs. My question in any conflicted situations is always: *"Why am I a player in this equation? What vibration is active in me to attract this? What meaning do I give to this? What is my part?"* It doesn't help to go into judgment or blame, or to create a story around it. *"What is my responsibility here? How can I change my story about this? What is the gift in this?"* I will typically ask.

In fact, it is more important to set clear energetic

boundaries first, so that you are not pushing against a behavior but rather coming to any situation from a posture of inner calm, clarity and centeredness. Rather than "trying" to protect yourself from outside energy, the best way to healthy energetic boundaries is to tend to your vibration first and then allow the boundaries to express themselves naturally and organically from the inside out.

Important part of healthy boundaries is to know when to say "no." Have you even said "yes," only to regret it right away? I know I have. When you honor yourself, you honor others. Speak your truth with integrity. Mean what you say. There is no need to overly explain. "No" is a complete sentence.

Remember also to clear any energy from the collective that exists in the situation. Send it back to the light by using a clearing statement from your daily energy hygiene routine, such as: *"I ask that any and all energy that is not mine, nor for my highest good, to be cleared, cleansed, and transmuted from my space now."*

Enter into your space of crystalline clarity, make a conscious choice of putting yourself first, pull yourself out of any limiting stories, commit to your truth and power. See yourself in your highest light. Then, walk to the world with confidence, compassion, peace, and love.

The Dance of Love Within You

Whether you are a man or a woman, there are both feminine and masculine aspects or frequencies within your being. When you tune into their highest frequency, any wounded parts can heal. We might call these highest aspects your divine or sacred self.

Imagine the divine feminine embodying the left side of your body and energy field, from head to toe filling your aura. Similarly imagine your right side fully embodied by the divine masculine. Imagine these two representations of your highest light as beautiful, powerful and luminous as you possibly can.

Imagine them, as a child would imagine them, looking into each other's eyes within you and recognizing each other's unique gifts and purpose. Imagine them seeing each other. Really seeing, like in the *Avatar* "I see you" kind of way. (If you haven't watched this movie yet, please do!) Feel how these two equal sides of you trust each other. They both feel seen and heard, honored and respected.

Imagine the masculine saying to the feminine: "*I love you. I am here to walk by your side, to hold sacred your extraordinary magical, mystical, creative, spiraling ways. I am here to guard your secrets and keep you safe. I am here for when you need me to act. I know how to make things happen. I plan and organize and find the perfect solution to bring your gifts to the world with clarity, courage and compassion. I don't pretend to understand you or your spiraling ways, but I will always honor and love you. Thank you for seeing me for who I am. I love you.*"

The feminine feels deeply received and seen and says: "*Thank you. I love you. I feel I can trust my mystical, magical ways with you. I feel your integrity, clarity, and love. Your outstanding gift to act is welcome. It resonates within my being. Thank you for so deeply understanding without the need to understand. I surrender to the love you offer as a container of our dreams. I weave my magic as you take inspired action. Together we are powerful. Together we are whole. Thank you for making me feel seen, honored and received. Thank you for being you."*

Check in with the divine couple, the true soulmates of your own soul, from time to time, so that you can be expanded and inspired by their solid commitment to each other. Imagine the divine couple complementing each other perfectly. Receive the unique gift each of them has for you. Feel their peace, balance, harmony, and love within your consciousness and in your heart.

If you wish to manifest a partner in the physical, before you do, become the lover and the beloved you wish to attract. Raise your own bar. Tend to your vibration and heal any old, unhealed wounds, so that you don't need to manifest a partner that reflects the wounds back to you. You want to attract someone who mirrors your wholeness. Then there is room for differences without it feeling threatening.

If you wish to improve an existing relationship, the same applies. Be in love, not in judgment. Know yourself. Know your needs and your values. Learn about your beloved's needs and values. Remember, they are most likely different from yours. Learn to value their love not to depend on it.

Be the spark you wish to ignite.

Have the courage to love more, not less.

Redeem Your Money Story

If the world reflected your beliefs about money, what would it look like? Would there be joyous abundance of money circulating? Would there be playful energy of ease and flow?

What is the meaning you give money? Our relationship with money doesn't depend on how much we have, or don't have, or on how much money someone else has, but rather on the meaning we give it, the story we tell. The story then becomes our personal reality. Life gives us what we are willing to settle for.

There is a new consciousness rising, a new story emerging—not only in the spiritual community, but in every field—where we are given the opportunity to pull ourselves out of the victim story, where we can shift from scarcity mindset to true abundance and flow. It is time for us to heal any past, present, or future story of lack and limitation. It is time money was included in our communion of oneness, love, joy, and freedom. We are all part of healing the energy of money and creating a new economy of empowerment, support and leadership of love.

Commit to an empowering story about money. Give it a joyous meaning. Receive it with gratitude, share it with gratitude. Bless your money and it blesses you. Love your money and it loves you. Imagine the amazing contribution you can make when your money works for goodness, kindness, inspiration and empowerment.

What if we allowed money to represent the highest energy of our highest values? For me it translates to authentic growth, greatest freedom, outstanding contribution, opportunity for all and infinite love. How about you?

If money were love, would you be a billionaire?

I say "yes" to that.

My Imaginary Manager

In my early years working as a freelance musician in New York City, I was living the story of the starving artist archetype. I had bought into the confusion around art and money, where artists are supposed to live by holy inspiration somehow and they are not considered "good" artists if they even so much as think about making money.

The same goes for energy healers and other "helpers." You are supposed to help people for free otherwise your contributions are not considered pure or you are accused of being selfish. There is almost a requirement of suffering and self-sacrifice in these stories, and it makes these compassionate career paths untenable for many people.

For years, I often found it difficult to set my prices for my solo performances, especially for my storytelling, entertaining, and healing one-woman shows. And when I did set a price, I was very quick to come down at the slightest sign of hesitance from a prospective client. There was a certain desperation at play; I was always afraid they would say no.

I felt guided to hire a manager, but not a human being, an imaginary one. I took a good part of one day to create a character who would be my manager. I had fun imagining how this person would be. It was like I was holding interviews for a job opening. His name was Abraham Goldberg. I figured that since in German *Goldberg* literally means "gold mountain," it must be good for business. He was a brilliant, silver-haired Jewish businessman from New York City. I knew down to my bones, if he could not sell my show, nobody could.

Abraham, Abe for short, who was a well-read true gentleman and a lover of the arts, was also very wealthy—a billionaire—so I knew he was not managing me to make money. He did it because he believed in the product: Me.

He began teaching me. We looked at my prices and my contracts. He helped me revise everything. Mind you, he was an imaginary person, yet I tapped into some very valuable information and advice through this character. He taught me how to value myself and how to value my creativity. He had me raise all my prices and to my great surprise and joy even clients that had tried to bargain before simply said: *"Send me the contract."*

Obviously, it was I who had the limiting story running in my brain. Consequently, my RAS and the Universe supported me in playing the starving artist role. It was easy for me, when thinking in that pattern, to blame the circumstances, the economy, the rich people, anything outside of me. I was the victim of my story.

Abe Goldberg, my wonderful manager, who drove a red Ferrari, had a villa and vineyard in Italy, showered me with inspiration, caring and compassion. He didn't judge me or blame me, he showed me a way of appreciating myself. With him behind me, I was not afraid anymore of a client saying no. If it happened, it was now just a no, not a rejection of me, my art, my work, my persona, or my heart.

Anchored in this new pattern of thought, I became excited to "sell" myself as a product, and I didn't feel like being taking advantage of anymore. All that was part of my old story.

When I was detached from the outcome, whether I was hired or not would not shake me. I started landing better paying performances with ease. Detachment was the key.

There are a couple of occasions that come to mind when I didn't want to travel quite so far for a very short performance, so I set the price so high (in my mind) that I was sure they'd say no, but then they ended up accepting without a blink. In both of those cases, not only was I paid really well and taken care of like royalty, but the jobs ended up being life changing in terms of meeting amazing people who would be very important to my personal development.

You can choose to stop feeding a limiting story anytime. The "starving artist" or any story of fear, lack or limitation can be reversed, not by society or our political leaders, but by you. The power is not out there; it is within each of us.

If we wait for any system to change, we remain victims of it forever. Success is not reserved only for a select few, we can have it too. But you must choose it, and to choose it, you must know what it means to you.

As we talked before, look for proof in stories of people who have persevered with their dreams and goals against different types of obstacles. Look for people who made a choice and a commitment to themselves, who pulled themselves out of a story of lack and poverty, and now are beacons of light for many, not only because of their money, but because of their spirit, freedom and massive contribution to a better and more beautiful world for everyone. If they can do it, so can you.

By the way, if you want, I can give you Abe's number.

Choosing Radiant Health: A Story of Healing

Inspired by one of my posts in a social network on our inner powers, my friend and colleague, the masterful Irish clarinetist Carol McGonnell wrote to me about her personal story. We ended up talking for a moment, and she gave me a permission to share her story with you. Carol is amazing musician. One of the rare ones. We used to play and premiere a lot of new music together in New York City back in the day.

About a year ago, Carol lost hearing in her left ear and, after trying steroids, which provided only temporary relief, the doctors said her hearing was gone. She was also told that when this particular condition happens in one ear, it eventually would happen in the other ear, and in some cases also affecting the eyes. So, it was just question of time before she would be entirely deaf, and possibly blind.

She was terrified. Couldn't sleep. Was thinking about her career ending. No more concerts. And she was panicking, thinking, *"This cannot be happening!"* Not only was she devasted about the implication for her career, but she would not be able to hear her children's voices. Everything in her life seemed to be sinking.

One morning, at the lowest point of her life, with no energy to get out of bed, she turned to Netflix and "happened" to notice the documentary *Heal,* a documentary by Kelly Noonan Gores, in which physicians and spiritual teachers take us on a scientific and spiritual journey on the power of the mind to heal the body. She clicked on it and began watching, even though she "knew" there was nothing to be done in her case. What struck her the most was watching the neuroscientist Dr. Joe Dispenza's account of his own miraculous recovery and complete healing from an injury when he had been told that he would never walk again. Carol bought a couple of his books and chose, decided, committed to healing her hearing by the time of her next appointment with her ear doctor. She had one month.

Carol is a mother of two small children, so she couldn't take an hour every day to meditate, but she began taking small moments here and there to meditate and focus her imagination with crystal-clear intention on the possibility of hearing perfectly with both ears. From Dr. Joe, she knew she couldn't be in fear. She had to change her state of being to where healing could happen. She had never meditated before, so she used her excellent skills as a world-class performer to find the absolute concentration and focus she needed, as well as drawing upon the feeling of joy that she draws from performing. She related this feeling of joy of performing with other musicians and imagining hearing them perfectly through both ears.

For those brief moments throughout the day that she was able to take for herself, she was easily, and quite rapidly able to find the zone she needed to drop into. She focused all her energy into hearing perfectly on the thirty-first of that month. Although she was a little worried periodically, she was able to raise herself back to focusing on crystal-clear hearing and the joy of playing so that the worry didn't have a chance to pull her down.

However, the real test came on the thirtieth of the month, the day before her exam. Her hearing hadn't improved much at all, and in her own words, her "ear still felt very broken." It was scary, but she chose to continue her meditations. She was determined not to give in or to give up. Her resolution was steadfast.

She decided that no matter what it took or how long it took, she was going to continue to meditate and focus her energy single mindedly on hearing perfectly in her left ear. She didn't care anymore if she met the "deadline" she had originally set for herself. All she cared about was keeping her vibration high and her focus crystal clear.

Come the thirty-first, Carol woke up with full and

complete recovery of hearing in her left ear. She danced her way to the exam. The doctors couldn't believe it because it was not supposed to happen. Carol was laughing when she told me: "Ulla, my hearing is actually better now in my left ear than my right." She was completely healed.

Would Carol's hearing have been restored if she gave up the day before? We shall never know, but I doubt it, as 99.99 percent of any healing, manifestation, or transformation is present in the vibrational reality before we see proof of it in the physical. Many people give up because they have seen no evidence of improvement yet. However, before giving up, we can all do what Carol did with clarity, conscious choice, and unwavering commitment. With healing, or any manifestation, there is no halfway. There is no trying or hoping. You either choose it or not.

The fact is, people are healing themselves of stage four cancer with zero percent chance to live according to their doctors. The same is true for multiple sclerosis, paralysis, and broken backs. You name it, people are healing it. Look for the evidence of miracles. When you begin to look, your consciousness begins to show you more. The signs are everywhere, and so are miracles.

Carol wrote to me recently: "Waking on the 31st to clear, perfect hearing was the greatest moment of my life, not just because I recovered my hearing, but because I realized the depth of possibilities we have as human beings. If I can inspire one person not to give up, it will give me such happiness."

The power of the Universe is within you. It creates through you. Choose to focus your energy, your thought and feeling so that you become greater than your limiting story, so that you become an extraordinary, unique, laser-like expression of the limitless consciousness of infinite possibility.

We Are World Peace, You and I Together

Biologically speaking, human beings share 99.9 percent of exactly the same DNA. While we keep creating separation through "racial" issues, we really don't have enough genetic differences between us even to substantiate categories for race. Other species of animal do. Banana flies, for example, have enough variations among them to scientifically differentiate "races," but we don't. How would it be if we just looked each other in the eye, and saw family?

Our children don't see differences; they naturally trust our sameness. Like in the story where a father asks his son after the first day of school, "Are there any foreigners in your class?" And the son responds, "No, in my class there are only children."

Once in Samarkand, Uzbekistan, I had just bought a bamboo flute from a local musician, when the group of musicians I was touring with from New York City visited the Mausoleum of Kusam-Ibn-Abbas, the tomb of Mohammed's cousin, a very sacred place for Muslims. We had a wonderful local guide, a young man who obviously loved his work, his culture, and his town.

When it was almost closing time, close to sunset, there were only three of us left in a simple space at the back of the mausoleum. All the other visitors including the rest of our group had already headed out. There was something mystical, magical about that space that spoke to me. The way light entered at that moment was as if the particles and waves were dancing and alchemizing in it. It felt as if the light was inviting my molecules to dance and be reorganized. I felt reverence in the space.

Sensing the sound of sacredness in the silence, I asked the young man from Samarkand if it would be okay for me to play my bamboo flute there. He said: "*I don't see why not, but please allow me to pray first. It is that time.*" He knelt down, facing Mecca, his beautiful voice echoed the prayers of centuries, his chant immersed in the light.

When he finished his prayer, I closed my eyes and brought the bamboo flute to my lips. I had just bought it, so I didn't know what sound would come out, but I chose to trust the moment. The first note of the flute into the silence, still resonating with the prayer, was exactly the note where he had left off.

I allowed the flute to lead the way and offered my heart through the flute into the dancing light. The flute drew a line in time, as if yearning to trace the prayer already sounded, then it gently merged back to the resounding silence.

Only later did I realize that together we represented the world peace, as there was the young Muslim man from

Samarkand, myself—a Nordic free spirit, raised in the Christian tradition—and a Jewish pianist, the leader of our new music group from New York City.

The seed of peace is in every moment, in every encounter. It is always there for you to see and to choose. The world we live in allows us to be closer to each other than ever before no matter where we are in the world. Let's support each other, let's meet each other with an open heart. Together we change the world.

Not in the future, but now.

I will treasure Samarkand as a sacred sign for peace and oneness. I will always remember the prayer in the dancing light.

PLAY WITH THE UNIVERSE

I invite you to look into your stories about love, money, health and your contribution to the world, and see if there are limiting stories or beliefs you are willing to release and replace with a higher vision for yourself. You don't have to be a victim, you can change today. Choose it with clarity and commitment. But first, is there anyone you would like to forgive?

Gentle Forgiveness: Visualization

Think of a person you would be willing to forgive. Imagine both of you in a safe space, perhaps in a healing temple, surrounded by a gentle healing light.

If you would like, you may imagine angels or other beings of the highest light holding space for both of you. See yourself in your highest light. See also the person in his or her highest light.

Say out loud:

"I choose to forgive you and set myself free.

I choose to forgive myself and set myself free.

I choose to forgive myself and let go of the story.

I choose to forgive you and let go of the story from my system now."

Imagine the person turning around and vanishing from your story like smoke in thin air.

See and feel yourself blessed by the divine angelic light. Say to yourself: *"I love you. Thank you."*

Radiant Health: Command Your Energy

Stand tall and breathe deeply. See yourself in perfect radiant health. Talk to your inner healer out loud with clarity, focus, and confidence:

Dear inner healer, I love you and I honor you.

I know you can perfectly heal, harmonize and balance my body, mind, emotion and spirit. I ask and command you to energize and optimize all my systems for total and complete radiant health and wellbeing.

Do it now.

Thank you, thank you, thank you.

At any time, you may also tap gently on your thymus

area to activate and boost your immune system. I like doing it at the same time I talk to my inner healer. You may talk to any part of your body. Command your own energy.

Journal to Shift Your Story

These questions are designed to give you clarity, so that you can focus your energies into interrupting limiting beliefs and focus your thought and energy to a better story. The Universe supports you whether you play small or big. You are loved whether you play small or big.

The question about how a limiting story might serve you might be surprising, but it is an important one, because it can reveal what you are trying to avoid, such as pain, rejection, disappointment, and such. It all depends on your values and the meaning you give to your stories and beliefs.

Your Love Story

See yourself with the eyes of love and compassion. These questions are not there to judge or to criticize, but to give you clarity and ultimately freedom to love and be loved.

- Do you love yourself? If yes, wonderful. If no, you just found your first limiting story.
- What are your top three limiting stories or beliefs of love?
- How do your limiting stories affect your life?
- What is the cost so far of your limiting stories or beliefs?

- How have your limiting stories served you?
- Who would you be without this story? Look at each story separately.
- Where do these stories come from?
- Are there any limiting beliefs about love that you have adopted from others?
- How important is love? What are you willing to risk?
- Are you moving towards love or away from love?
- What is your greatest fear about love?
- What action are you willing to take to clear the fear?
- What is your highest vision of love for you? Write in detail about loving yourself as well as romantic love, family love and universal love.
- What needs to shift for you to live your highest vision of love?
- How would your life change if your life reflected your highest vision of love?
- What action do you choose today to shift your story of love?
- Who would you choose to be your love role model?
- Tap on any limiting feeling about love.

Your Highest Vision of Money

Money is energy just like everything else in the world. By clearing your money stories, you help clear other people's similar stories. Remember, when you shift, the world shifts.

- What are your top three limiting money stories?

- How do your limiting stories affect your life?
- Are you telling someone else's story about money? Whose story is it?
- What is the cost of your limiting money story?
- How have you benefitted from your limiting story?
- Who would you be without this story?
- If you had $10,000,000, what would you do? How would you use it?
- Who would you help? How would it feel?
- What does success mean to you in terms of money?
- What is the meaning you give money?
- What belief or story about money are you willing to release?
- What is your highest vision of money for you?
- What must change for you to live your highest vision of money?
- How would your life change if you committed to your highest vision of money? Look at different areas of your life.
- Who would you choose to be your financial role model? Who inspires you?
- Whose values do you respect, who also has a lot of money? How do they contribute to the world?
- What action are you willing to commit to today to shift your story about money?
- How would your future be different if you committed today?

Your Health and Wellness Story

When you are healthy everything flows easier, but we often stop to appreciate health only after we lose it. When you imagine yourself radiantly healthy, and thank every part of your miraculous body, you boost all of your systems and summon your body's innate healing abilities.

- What are your top three limiting beliefs about your health? And health in general? Think deep.
- How is your overall energy? How is your diet? Do you get enough quality sleep?
- What does health mean to you? How important is wellbeing for you?
- Is there an area of wellness where you are willing to change? Is there something you must change?
- How would your whole life benefit from shifting your story about health and wellness?
- What is the cost of not choosing? What is the benefit of not choosing?
- What belief do you need to release to make the choice?
- What is your highest vision for yourself in terms of health and wellness? Write in detail.
- Who inspires you in terms of wellness? Why?
- What action are you willing to take to shift your story about health and wellness?
- How would your future change if you committed to your highest vision of health today?

Your Vision for the World

There is always room for a higher vision through which your contribution can be bigger and your actions more impactful.

Free yourself to change your life and the world through your conscious choices. Every choice counts.

- Are there any limiting stories about the world that are pulling you down or making you feel helpless?
- How are these stories serving you?
- What choices can you make to release and replace them?
- If the world reflected your values, what would it be like?
- How can you bring the essence of what you value the most into the world?
- What needs to shift for you to believe that you can make a difference?
- What are you willing to do to shift it?
- What is your highest vision for your contribution to the world? Who could be your role model?
- What action are you willing to choose and commit to now? How can you contribute now?
- How would the world change if you committed today?
- How can you raise the bar higher for yourself?
- Who could be your role model in making a difference in the world?

Instant Shift Tips

Here are four different kind of instant shift actions you can take to embody your highest energy, to awaken and energize your body, and to bless the world.

Choose a technique of the week from all the instant shift techniques, or invent your own. It is good to have an idea for when you need to stop, reset and reprogram. Keep it simple. Smile.

Go for a Walk as Your Highest Vision

The way you move is the way you feel. See yourself in your highest light. Go for a walk as your highest vision. Walk into the world as confident, tall, happy, radiant, curious, or as any other kind of state of being that has the highest meaning for you. Condition yourself to walk as success, luminosity, creativity, abundance, or joy. Walk into the world as if the world was blessing you, as if the world was your beloved.

Instant Awakening

Finish your shower with ice cold water.

You will have an instant activation of energy and stimulation of your lymphatic system, which not only drains your body of toxins, but transports the infection-fighting white blood cells everywhere in your body.

A swim in cold water or a cold shower is a great way to begin your day or to reset at any time.

I come from Finland, where in the winter we dip into a hole in a frozen lake. Many do this without sauna, but others like me, rather go to the freezing water from a hot sauna and afterwards run back as quickly as possible.

While the actual moment of entering the ice-cold water is quite extreme, the feeling afterwards is pure bliss. According to many studies, the health benefits of *avanto* (the hole in the frozen lake in Finnish) include improved circulation and metabolism of your tissues, stimulation of the lymph system and strengthening of the heart. So, if there is no frozen lake around, do it in your shower.

Sing a Song: Every Little Cell in My Body is Happy

Perhaps you know this song, if not, make your own version, or go to my website to hear it (see Resources for details).

Celebrate your cells, celebrate your body. Sing and dance. Be playful and silly.

First part. "Every little cell in my body is happy
Every little cell in my body is well."(repeat)

Second part. "I'm so glad, 'cause every little cell
In my body is happy and well." (repeat)

As You Bless, You Are Blessed

Bless everyone and everything you encounter. Bless people, trees, animals, flowers, clouds, rocks.

Look at everything with the eyes of love and compassion. It shifts the way you see the world.

When you bless, you are blessed.

Say silently, in your mind, something simple that feels natural to you. You may want to outline your blessing in your journal.

I say it now to you, wherever you are in the world: *"I see you in your highest light. May you be infinitely blessed. I love you. Thank you."*

Your Wisdom Book

Draft any of your gratitude statements in your other journal. Write the most empowering and inspiring gems down in your wisdom book.

- Write your most powerful gratitude statements on love, money, health and world peace in your wisdom book.
- Find quotes on love, money, health and world peace.
- Write your most important insights from this chapter.
- Keep filling your wisdom book with meaningful thoughts and ideas.

NINE

YOU ARE THE UNIVERSE

Be still and listen to the wisdom of your heart. Have
courage to love and to live in the present moment. Fear
not. Be healed and be blessed. Pass it on.

C ommit to seeing yourself in your highest light. Make
it a habit to see, feel, and envision yourself as happy,
strong, radiantly healthy, at peace, filled with light, and in
love with life. Honor your commitment day by day, moment
by moment. Imagine breathing as the earth—receive the
anchoring, grounding energy of the earth. Be one with the
earth energy that supports you, nurtures you, listens to you,
hears you, feels you, and receives you with every step you
take.

Play with the Universe. Choose light and lightness.
Allow the energy that creates worlds to flow through you
and create as you. You are the Universe, and the Universe
is you.

Appreciate your signs as part of your truth and part of
your natural, organic communion and communication with

the Universe, through consciousness as consciousness.

Trust yourself. Trust life. Trust the Universe.

If you are the Universe and the Universe is everything, what can you possibly lack?

Embrace the greatness in you. Embody the infinite possibility. Direct your energy consciously, exuberantly and joyously. Reclaim your freedom. You are a unique spark of creation, an important frequency in the symphony of the whole, wholeness and holiness.

Choose and commit, keep choosing and committing. Elevate your vibration and follow the essence of your dreams all the way to fulfillment. Only you can stop you.

Say out loud: *"I invite all the parts of me into this infinite now, cleared, cleansed, healed, and harmonized, deeply blessed with the energy and vibration of love, abundance, and infinite possibility and potentiality."*

Allow a deep, loving breath as you receive the light of the Universe that activates and energizes your entire system. Soften your heart gently. Tune in to your infinite, eternal livingness right where the earth and the heavens meet, at the still point of your inbreath and outbreath.

See with the eyes of love, magic and possibility.

Acknowledge the miracle you are.

Say out loud: *"I let go of everything that is not mine—anything and everything that doesn't serve me at this moment. I choose to be free. I choose to be whole and complete as I am. I am my own wisdom, truth and light. I am my own permission, validation and approval to choose and to commit with clarity, courage and* consciousness. *I love, honor, and accept myself deeply and completely as I am."*

Do you recall the dolphin on my vision board that led me to Hawaii? I am writing this book because of the dolphin. It was a sign that I followed. It was on Lanikai Beach in Kailua, on the island of Oahu, where I spoke to the Universe, asking for a TEDx Talk. The next day, I received an email from Eric Ladd of Outlaw Partners in Big Sky, Montana, asking if I was interested in being one of their speakers in their TEDx series. You may have seen the talk "Do You See the Signs of the Universe?" that I consequently presented. That talk might have even prompted you to read this book. And it's all because I followed the dolphin.

When choosing my topic for this talk, I had so many ideas, but the idea of signs of the Universe kept nudging me.

I even said to the Universe, *"Let me do something else, because I have talked so much about signs."*

"That is exactly why you will talk about signs now," came the answer.

I am grateful to the signs for bringing me all the way here so that now I can hold space for you to learn to read your signs and shift your story, and so that you may choose with clarity and commitment to follow the nudges that beckon you to expand into healing, wholeness, peace, and possibility.

During the time of writing this book, I had asked for a

sign after a bit of a tough day. In the evening as I was getting ready to talk to my mom on the phone, I felt I needed to shift my state of being first, because I know I cannot hide my feelings from her and I don't want to worry her. So, I did some gentle bouncing, shifted my posture, put a smile on my face, and asked the angels to hold space for both of us.

Almost immediately after she answered the phone, she said: *"Wait, a piece of paper just fell out of a book."* Then she went on to read it to me in Finnish: *"May you walk with joy and light today. Remember, angels are always with you. Request, ask, be thankful. Breathe deeply, open your heart to the beauty and the support of the Universe. Allow the blessings of light to fill you to the brim and overflow. Shine your light fearlessly. With love, your daughter Ulla."* It was a handwritten message I had written to her years ago, perhaps ten to fifteen years ago, when she was having a rough day. Now she read it to me exactly when I needed it.

With tears flowing of gratitude, I indeed was filled to the brim and overflowing. This showed me how signs of the Universe can be recycled and how we can be messengers not only for each other, but even for ourselves, or our future selves.

I now invite you to shine your light fearlessly, so that you dare to dream big, shake off any "shoulds," shift any "I can't" into "yes, I can, and I choose it now!"

Set the bar high, and higher, because you can.

It doesn't necessarily mean bigger or greater, but rather

more genuine and authentic. It means knowing yourself and being true to yourself. You are greater than you think.

Ask yourself: *"What is the price of not choosing, or the cost of believing in limitation?"*

Let's not just hope for the best, let's *be* the best.

Shift your state of being, focus your energy with crystalline clarity, say "yes!" to yourself and to your highest vision. Allow the highest consciousness of the Universe to flow through you and to inform your form, so you know and trust yourself as the Universe, then, not only do you see the signs, but—you are a sign—a luminous sign of the Universe.

ACKNOWLEDGEMENTS

Dearest reader, I am grateful to you. With you, the creation of this book completes itself.

I am grateful to my mother, *Eeva Suokko,* for being my greatest fan and for continuing to hold space for me. I appreciate it now more than ever.

Thank you to my father, *Kalervo Suokko,* for the gift of the musical genes and for playing an important role in my personal journey of transformation. A journey that led to me becoming a transformational coach and helping people all over the world. I am grateful for the connection we have today.

Thank you also to my brother, *Matti Suokko,* who I admire for always finding brilliant, practical solutions. I am inspired by his business sense, manifesting skills, and ease with money.

Without the opportunity to give a TEDx Talk in Big Sky, Montana, this book might not have been written. Thank you, *Eric Ladd,* for following your gift of seeing possibilities and inviting me to speak. I am grateful for the generous spirit of the whole team at TEDx Big Sky, fronted by *Erzin Ozer.*

In Big Sky, I received invaluable and treasured support from my dear dragon sister *Mary Casey Ladd* and her husband, *Tom Levar.* They surprised me by flying in from Minnesota. Thank you for being my dream team.

A special thank you goes to "Coach Jackie," *Jackie Corcoran,* whose wise and caring guidance helped me shape my talk. Jackie was also my go-to sounding board for planning this book. Thank you for allowing me to talk in circles until I became clear.

I am grateful for the countless messages and questions from from all of you who have viewed the TEDx Talk and from all my wonderful clients, you are an integral part of the birth of this book.

Thank you, *Carol McGonnell,* outstanding artist and human being, for allowing me to tell your story. Thank you, *Micaela Preguerman,* for lending me your expert eyes and giving me valuable support and feedback on my cover design. Thank you, *Mirkku Merimaa,* for an inspiring photoshoot in Helsinki, and for seeing me and capturing the moment for my author photo.

Thank you, *Stephanie Gunning,* for being my editor and accomplice in creating my first book all the way from the idea to publishing it. You pushed me to be on track with deadlines, and gave me space when it was needed. English not being my first language, you expertly cared for my language, fully preserving my voice and way of expression. (Any mistakes or confusions are completely mine, not hers.)

My deep gratitude goes to my dear friend, *Kathy Surles,* for steadfastly seeing me in my highest light throughout the years. I know can fully trust that I will be seen, accepted, and held in an unconditional space of truth, healing, and love by her.

I want to acknowledge my dear friend *Gerry Henkel,* whose kantele I stole and then we became friends for life! He also builds the best saunas. (Harder to steal.) Thank you, Gerry, for your genius of connecting people, for always looking for deeper truths and for your wisdom to listen.

Thank you to another dear friend *Susanna Mälkki,* for being an inspiring example of embracing excellence and outstanding success in such a natural, elegant and organic way. I am grateful for our heartfelt conversations, the laughs and cries, and the seamless connection which began many years ago in Jorma Panula's sauna, and continues no matter where we are in the world.

I am forever grateful for each encounter during my years in New York City. Thank you, *Victorio,* for teaching *arte* through flamenco, *Sensei Robert Hodes,* for the life lessons through karate. My gratitude goes to my dear friend *Susan Meyer,* who took me in when I didn't know where to go.

Thank you to all my Juilliard professors, especially to the legendary flutist *Julius Baker,* who showed me the way to trust myself as an artist. I am also grateful to all my peers I met over the years across the freelance music scene in NYC. Thank you, New York, for showing me who I can be.

Muchas gracias, my beloved Peru, especially Cusco, Machu Picchu, Lima, and Mancora, for helping me remember an important piece of my soul. Thank you, *Mamacocha,* the great Pacific Ocean. Thank you, *Pachamama* and the great *Apus* of the Andes, especially mountain

Putukusi, for opening my crystalline connection to the stars. Thank you, *Jesús Eagle,* for always being able to count on you. Thank you, *Benito Quispe,* for showing me the way of seeing the good signs. Thank you, *Adriana Peralta,* for magical photos and important sisterhood. Urpillay sonqollay, *Señor Feliciano* and your whole family for adopting me as part of the family and for looking after my home during my travels.

Thank you, *Jorge Garrido-Lecca* and *Bea Morachimo,* for embracing me in ERART family. Thank you, *Yvonne Von Mollendorff,* for always setting the bar(re) high.

Aloha *Michelle Pillen* and *Teresa Iwashita,* thank you for a magical, mystical, life-changing journey through earth, wind, fire, water and music in Oahu and the Big Island of Hawaii.

Thank you, Finland, for infusing me with a natural connection to the earth, trees, animals, crystals, lakes, fairies, and—silence. Thank you to Italy, my lifelong inspiration and love affair. The cover of this book is a blurred photo I took of a Mediterranean sunset from the island of Capri.

I am grateful for having followed my dream of traveling the world, studying with outstanding people and meeting extraordinary souls who have deeply touched my soul. Thank you, every single one of you, whether or not you are mentioned by name. I will remain in love with all of you for the rest of my life, no matter where my path takes me next.

RESOURCES

If you're interested in going deeper into your studies of signs and shifting your story, here are some additional resources.

Take My Classes and Courses
Please visit my website: https://signsoftheuniverse.com.
Please also join the Signs mailing list.

Join Me on the Social Networks
Join our private Facebook group.
https://facebook.com/groups/signsoftheuniverse

Follow me on Instagram for inspiration.
https://www.instagram.com/ullasuokko

Subscribe to my YouTube channel.
https://www.youtube.com/ullasuokko

Listen to My Guided Meditations
https://wisewomanenergetics.com/signs-meditations

Watch My Instant Shift Tips Videos
https://wisewomanenergetics.com/signs-instant-shift-tips

Watch My Tapping for Emotional Freedom Videos
https://wisewomanenergetics.com/signs-eft

ABOUT THE AUTHOR

ULLA SUOKKO

In addition to being an international concert artist with a doctoral degree from The Juilliard School, Ulla Suokko is a transformational coach, reiki master, light ascension teacher, VortexHealing® practitioner, intuitive sound healer, and owner of a spiritual empowerment business, WiseWoman.

She is on a mission to guide thousands of people from all over the world to reclaim their power, joy, peace, and freedom in order to create a better future for all humanity and the planet.

A consummate storyteller and speaker, Ulla's TEDx Talk "Do You See the Signs of the Universe?" has had more than a million views. *Signs of the Universe* is her first book.

Made in the USA
Columbia, SC
15 December 2020

28296970R00126